HOW TO CREATE AN
HEIRLOOM QUILT

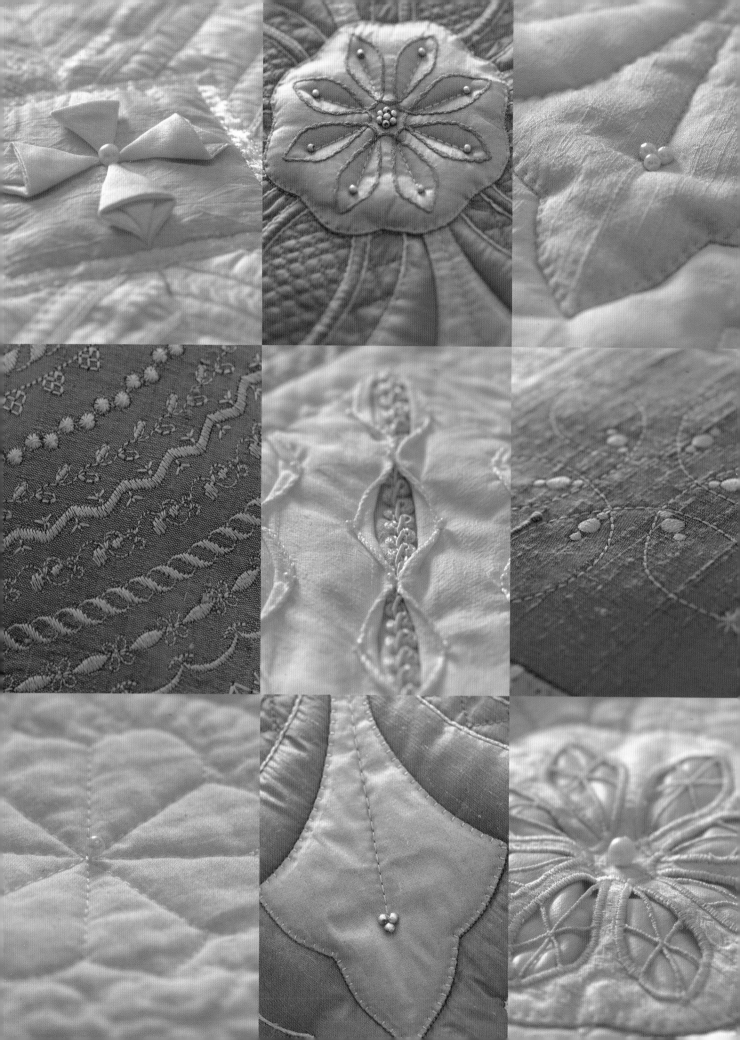

HOW TO CREATE AN HEIRLOOM QUILT

Learn over 35 machine techniques to build a beautiful quilt

PAULINE INESON

David and Charles

This book is dedicated to my very dear friends, Carol, Claire, Dauna, Jan and Margaret in Los Angeles, whose American attitude – that you can do anything if you put your mind to it – has rubbed off on me.

I also dedicate it to the ladies I teach at Sytchampton, especially those in the first two Heirloom Quilt classes, who had faith in my design and started the quilt before I had finished it myself. They are doing the same with my appliqué quilt, but that's another story – or another book!

A DAVID & CHARLES BOOK
Copyright © David & Charles Limited 2010

David & Charles is an F+W Media Inc. company
4700 East Galbraith Road, Cincinnati, OH 45236

First published in the UK and US in 2010

Text and designs copyright © Pauline Ineson 2010
Layout and photography copyright © David & Charles 2010

Pauline Ineson has asserted her right to be identified as author of this work in accordance with the Copyright, Designs and Patents Act, 1988.

A catalogue record for this book is available from the British Library.

ISBN-13: 978-0-7153-3525-3 paperback
ISBN-10: 0-7153-3525-1 paperback

Printed in China by RR Donnelley
for David & Charles
Brunel House   Newton Abbot   Devon

Commissioning Editors Jane Trollope and Cheryl Brown
Assistant Editor Juliet Lines
Project Editor Lin Clements
Design Manager Sarah Clark
Photographers Sian Irvine and Joe Giacomet
Diagrams Ethan Danielson
Production Controller Kelly Smith
Pre Press Jodie Culpin and Natasha Jorden

David & Charles publish high quality books on a wide range of subjects. For more great book ideas visit:
www.rubooks.co.uk

Contents

Introduction

I remember the first time I used a wing needle, inserted lace and did circular sewing on a course designed to show me how to use my new sewing machine – I was hooked! I had been dressmaking for years but this new form of machine sewing just blew me away. It was creative, exciting, fun and opened up a whole new world. I spent hours researching and developing the many techniques you will find in this book. The Heirloom Quilt is a culmination of these, a sort of encyclopaedia of techniques, brought to life in a stunning quilt.

The Heirloom Quilt design took many forms, starting with twenty squares each incorporating a different technique. This changed to a crazy patch design but fortunately I hadn't started sewing at this point. It was whilst I was on holiday in Venice that the design suddenly came together and previous ideas were abandoned. The shell shapes and centres of many of the blocks are based on the beautiful architecture I found in this part of Italy.

I developed the quilt not only to explore these techniques for myself but to teach them to my ladies at Sytchampton, where I run classes on all forms of creative machine sewing. I therefore needed it to be easy enough for my class to produce a quilt they would be proud of and become an heirloom, whilst learning how to get the most from their machines. I decided to construct it in a similar way to a 'quilt as you go' method, by quilting the wadding (batting) to each block, cutting it to size and then joining each block together. This way, everything fits! The quilt was then backed and stitched in the ditch before the borders were added. This method makes the quilting process much easier as the intricate quilting is done before joining it together.

With the basic design in my head and the first few blocks made, my ladies couldn't wait for me to finish before teaching them, so off we all went to buy the silk and Heirloom Quilt 1 class was started. I am now on Heirloom Quilt 7 and keep saying that this one is the last! At least now when I am asked to start another one I can say, 'Buy the book!'. To this date about seventy ladies have made or are in the process of making the quilt.

I entered the quilt in the Festival of Quilts show at the NEC in Birmingham, UK and was thrilled that it was juried into the Quilts 2007 group. It then went on to win a first for Machine Quilting, a first for Patchwork and Quilting, a second in The Bed Quilt category and a Judges' Choice from Sandie Lush at Quilts UK, Malvern. This gave me the incentive to enter it in the International Quilt Festival in Houston, USA, where it was awarded an Honourable Mention.

Many people use their sewing machines for only basic sewing and are not really sure what else it can do. This book is written in the hope that you will get to know more about your sewing machine, learn all about the lovely techniques featured in the Heirloom Quilt and create a fabulous heirloom quilt of your own, which will be treasured for many years to come. You will also be able to incorporate the techniques into designs and projects of your own.

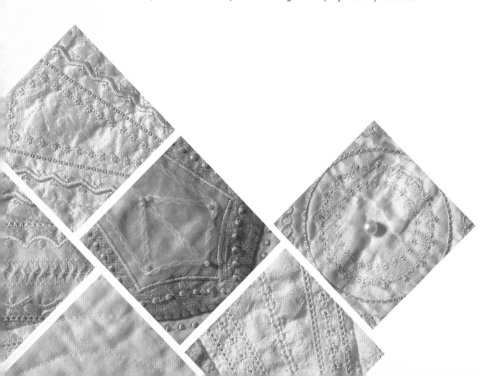

Using This Book

- The Heirloom Quilt was made using Imperial measurements. Metric equivalents have been given but the best results will be obtained using Imperial inches and yards.
- Some blocks occur twice or more in the Heirloom Quilt: generally, the block instructions are for making one block, so repeat to make as many blocks as needed.

This layout diagram of the quilt shows the position of all the blocks and the borders in the Heirloom Quilt

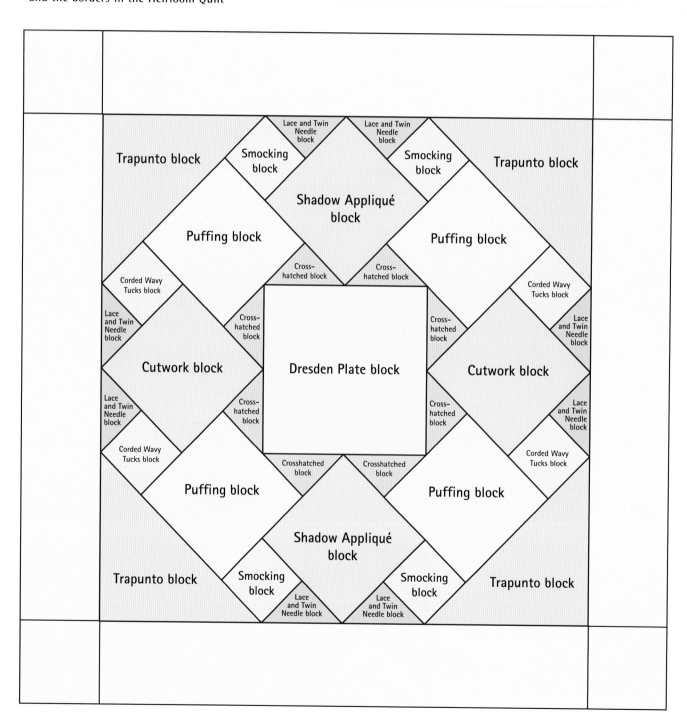

- The You Will Need lists tell you what requirements you will need to make one block. If making two, four or eight blocks, these requirements will need to be multiplied accordingly.
- Most of the chapters also have a smaller project, which you could make first in order to practise the techniques.
- The step-by-step instructions are full and detailed and include diagrams and detail pictures to make it even easier to complete your quilt.
- Templates are required for some blocks. Wherever possible these have been provided at full size but some have been reduced to fit the page size – simply check the template label to see what percentage the template needs to be enlarged by.
- Diagrams are provided throughout to assist you. WS = wrong side of fabric; RS = right side of fabric.
- If you are unsure as to whether your sewing machine will be able to sew the Heirloom Quilt see the box on page 102 for advice. There is also useful advice on sewing machine feet on page 104.
- All of the techniques used for the quilt are described and illustrated on pages 102–142.

A combination of couched cord, trapunto and beads makes a wonderful centre motif for an elegant cushion.

Three delicate shades of silk create the gorgeous tulip shapes for the Puffing blocks in the Heirloom Quilt.

Materials and Equipment

The general materials needed to make the quilt are described here briefly but refer to the You Will Need lists in each block for specific details of requirements. The main piece of equipment you will need is your sewing machine – see pages 102–104 for lots of useful advice and the answers to questions you might have.

Sewing Machine

You will be surprised at how many of the techniques in this book can be done using a basic sewing machine. Many techniques require only straight and zigzag stitch, although a machine with a selection of decorative stitches is preferable. The book will also teach you how to get the most out of a more advanced machine, if you have one.

Fabrics

I used silk dupion in different shades of coffee and cream for the Heirloom Quilt, but you could choose any colour in three or four different shades or even dye your own. It does not necessarily have to be silk, although I do think it needs to be a natural fibre.

A good quality calico was used for the background and backing as I like the contrast of the silk and calico. I used 100% cotton for the wadding (batting). If you plan to wash the finished quilt (*not* something I'd recommend!) then you will need to pre-wash your fabrics.

Linen is used for the pulled thread work on the central Dresden Plate block and organza (silk or polyester) for all the shadow appliqué areas. Four lace motifs are required for each Cutwork block.

Needles and Threads

Sewing machine needles you will require include Universal 70 or Embroidery 75 and Quilting needles. You will also need a wing needle and a twin needle.

For threads I used 30 and 40 weight rayon machine embroidery thread, thread for the bobbin and 50 weight machine sewing thread. The rayon threads used for the decorative stitching were in similar shades to the silk. Cotton or polyester threads were used for quilting and sewing the blocks together.

Delicate petal-shaped cutwork with Richelieu bars looks fabulous, especially with a pearl bead in the centre.

The cathedral windows technique looks beautiful with pretty braid peeping through and cord couched on the edges.

Stabilizers

You will need fine, double-sided fusible interfacing for some areas of the quilt, such as Steam-A-Seam2 or Bondaweb (Wonder Under) and fine fusible interfacing, such as Vilene. Tear-away stabilizer and water-soluble stabilizer are also needed – see page 122 for more advice.

Fabric Markers

Everyone has their favourite type of fabric marker but the best ones I have found are the air-erasable or iron-erasable ones. The air-erasable ones disappear after a period of time (check the manufacturer's instructions), so make sure that you can complete the work needed before the marks disappear. Iron-erasable markers are removed by the heat of an iron. Take care though as some markers, such as water-soluble ones, can actually be set by the heat of an iron. Always test your marker on scrap fabric first. You might also find a hera useful for marking fabric. This is a small hand tool that can be used to make a crease in fabric.

Other Materials

- A rotary cutter, mat and quilter's ruler are useful for cutting the fabric needed for each block and for cutting the blocks to size before making up.
- Cotton edging lace is needed for the Shadow Appliqué block.
- Cords are used in the quilt for additional embellishment and these can be rayon or cotton stranded and/or twisted cords.
- Piping was used in the quilt (size 4mm). You could buy this ready-made but it's very easy to make your own – see page 141 for instructions.
- Beads in various sizes have been used in the quilt. These are optional but they do add an extra opulent quality to the quilt.

11

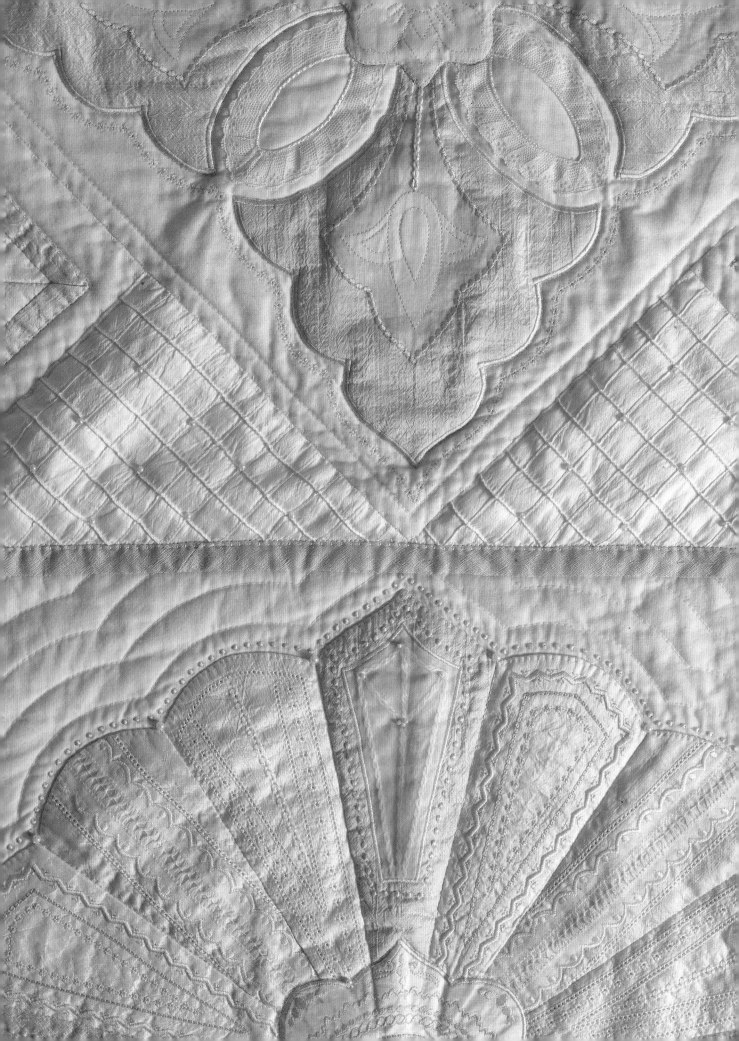

Making
the blocks

Dresden Plate Block

The Dresden Plate block makes up the impressive centre of the Heirloom Quilt. It is composed of four wing needle petals, four decorative petals, four pulled thread petals, four pointed petals and the centre appliqué – all of which are described in detail in this section. The templates required are given full size on pages 28–29. If you want to try some of the techniques in a small project first then turn to page 24 and make the lovely nine-patch cushion.

Finished size of block: 21in x 21in (53.3cm x 53.3cm) includes ½in (1.3cm) seam allowance for quilt assembly

Techniques: wing needle sewing (page 112) • decorative stitching (page 106) • pulled thread sewing (page 114) • chain stitching (page 105) • satin stitch appliqué (page 116) • candlewicking by machine (page 113) • circular sewing (page 110) • finished-edge appliqué (page 114)

tip

Heat-resistant plastic is a good material for creating the petal templates as you can see the drawing marks through it. If using thin card, the easiest way is to photocopy the shape straight on to the card.

Preparing the Petal Templates

1 Cut a piece of fusible interfacing 9in x 32in (22.8cm x 81.3cm) and iron this on to the wrong side of the light silk. Make a template of the rounded petal pattern given on page 28 (Template 1a) in either thin card or heat-resistant template plastic. Mark the dashed lines at the sides and the dotted line at the top on to the template and cut it out on the solid, outer line. Draw around the template eight times on the back of the interfaced silk and cut the shapes out on the outer line (see Fig 1 below for layout). Four of these will be used for the decorative petals and four for the wing needle petals.

Fig 1

2 Now make a pattern of the facing with the rounded top, Template 2a on page 29 and use this to cut out eight facings from the non-interfaced light silk. Put these to one side.

- Light silk ¼yd (0.25m) x 45in (115cm) wide
- Medium silk ¼yd (0.25m) x 45in (115cm) wide
- Dark silk ¼yd (0.25m) x 45in (115cm) wide
- Organza 6in x 12in (15.2cm x 30.5cm)
- Linen or loosely woven cotton 8in (20.3cm) square
- Calico or background fabric 24in (61cm) square
- Wadding (batting) 24in (61cm) square
- Medium or fine fusible interfacing ½yd (0.5m) x 36in (91.5cm) wide
- Fusible web such as Bondaweb (Wonder Under) 6in (15.2cm) square
- Tear-away stabilizer
- Decorative cord for chain stitching, such as two-ply rayon cord or stranded cotton embroidery thread 6yd (6m) approximately
- 40 tiny pearl beads (3mm–4mm diameter) and one larger bead (4mm–6mm diameter)
- Threads: rayon machine embroidery thread 40 weight to match dark silk; rayon machine embroidery thread 40 weight to match light silk; machine thread for bobbin and machine thread to match linen for sewing the petals together
- Machine needle size 60 or 70 and a wing needle
- Open-toe foot
- Adhesive electrical tape 4in (10.2cm) long
- Masking tape 5in (12.7cm) x ¼in (6mm) wide
- Heat-resistant template plastic (preferable) or thin card
- Drawing pin with a flat head
- Air-erasable marking pen or chalk marker

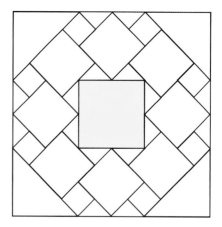

Position of the Dresdon Plate block in the Heirloom Quilt

3 Using the medium shade silk and 9in x 18in (22.8cm x 45.7cm) of fusible interfacing, repeat steps 1 and 2 and cut out four petals and four facings. These will be used for the pulled thread petals.

4 Using the dark silk and 9in x 18in (22.8cm x 45.7cm) of fusible interfacing, the pointed petal pattern Template 1b on page 28 and pointed facing Template 2b, repeat steps 1 and 2 and cut out four petals and four facings. These will be used for the pointed petals.

5 Now cut the rounded and pointed petal templates on the dashed line at the sides. Do not cut anything from the top edge. This is the finished size of the petals at the sides with ¼in (6mm) seam allowance added at the top edge. Place this template on the wrong side of one of the petals so that the top edge lines up with the top edge of the silk and there is the same amount of fabric protruding either side. Iron the edges over the template to mark the seam lines. Remove the template and fold the petal shape in half lengthways. Press to form a crease, marking the centre of the shape. You will now have creases to mark the outer finished shape and the centre, as in Fig 2. These will be used as guides for the stitching. Repeat for all the other petals.

Sewing the Wing Needle Petals

1 On four of the rounded top petals in light silk, draw a line with a removable marker on the right side ¼in (6mm) below the top raw edge.

2 Read Wing Needle Sewing on page 112 before you begin these petals. Use a similar colour top thread to the silk, insert a wing needle and set your machine to stop with the needle down if you can. Open out the sides of the petals flat, so they are not sewn down, and place tear-away stabilizer underneath. Select a small entredeux stitch or similar (see Fig 3) and begin at the bottom of a petal, sewing towards the top edge. Line the inside edge of the foot against the side seam crease. Just before you reach the corner, stop at the end of the stitch pattern (use the 'Pattern End' or 'Stop' function on your machine, if you have it) and pivot so that the edge of the foot is on the drawn

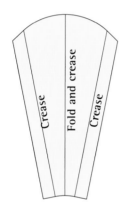

Fig 2

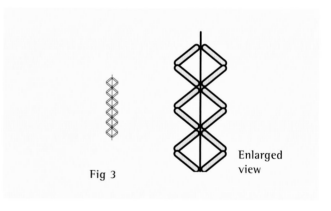

Fig 3

Enlarged view

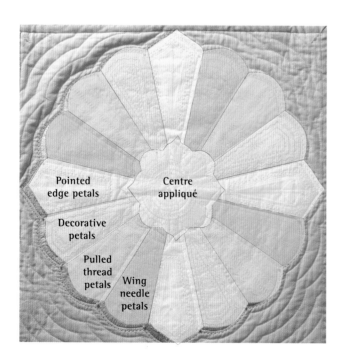

The Dresden Plate in the centre of the Heirloom Quilt is composed of four wing needle petals, four decorative petals, four pulled thread petals, four pointed petals and the centre appliqué, all identified here.

line at the top. Sew along the top to the next corner, stopping again at the end of a stitch pattern. Pivot and sew down the other side (Fig 4). Cut or carefully tear away the stabilizer after each row of stitching.

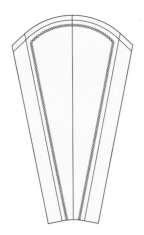

Fig 4

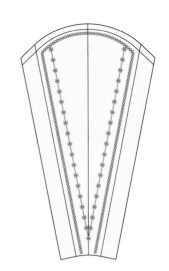

Fig 7

3 Select another stitch that is designed to be used with a wing needle – a motif one, such as a star or cross stitch, works well (see also Tip below). Begin at the bottom of the centre crease, ½in (1.3cm) above the cutting line. Sew one pattern (Fig 5). With the needle in the down position, pivot the petal so that the foot is pointing towards the top. Line the previous row of stitching next to or just under the right toe of the foot and sew towards the top, stopping just below the previous row of stitching under the top edge (Fig 6). For the other side, begin again at the bottom, placing the needle opposite the stitch pattern on the first side and sew towards the top as before (Fig 7).

4 Now select the same stitch you used for the first row. Begin at the top just below the first row of stitching with the foot pointing towards the bottom edge of the petal. Sew down the right side, keeping the previous row of stitches under the right toe of the foot. Stop and secure when you reach the centre crease. Repeat for the left side, keeping the left toe of the foot on the previous row of stitches.

5 Select another wing needle stitch. Begin just below the first row of stitching along the top edge. Sew down the centre crease, stopping when you reach the point where the gap is too narrow to fit another pattern (Fig 8).

tip
When choosing stitches for wing needle sewing you may decide to make the stitch narrower and shorter, in which case adjust the stitch length and width accordingly, and practise first!

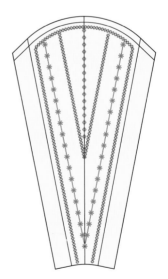

Fig 8

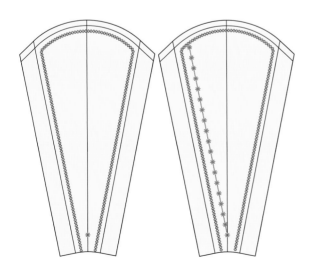

Fig 5   Fig 6

6 Sew the facing, right sides together to the top edge of the petal using a ¼in (6mm) seam allowance. Do not sew down the sides of the petal. Trim the seam and fold the facing over to the wrong side of the petal. Press the seam edge.

7 Now repeat this procedure (steps 2–6 above) to sew the remaining three wing needle petals. Place the petals to one side for the moment until they are needed later.

corner. Pivot, continue along the top edge, pivot at the next corner and then sew down the other side. If using this method, practise first to make sure that the stitch patterns are the same at both corners.

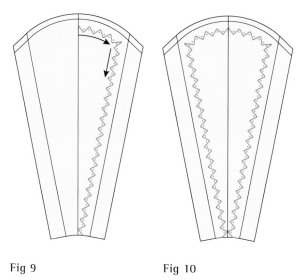

Fig 9   Fig 10

Sewing the Decorative Petals

1 On the remaining four rounded top petals in light silk, draw a line ¼in (6mm) below the top raw edge using a removable marker. Read Decorative Stitching page 106 before you begin sewing, paying particular attention to the tips and pictures on sewing patterns at a corner. See also the Tip below. The first row of stitches is sewn in two stages, each starting at the centre along the top edge and then going down the side.

tip   Creating the decorative petals is an opportunity to use some of your favourite stitches. Before deciding on the stitches to use, practise first on a scrap of fabric cut to the petal shape. Satin stitch patterns look best because they are bolder and show up better, however, if you don't have many of these use a thicker 30 weight thread that will show up well on an open/delicate pattern. Not all decorative stitches look good at a corner, which is why it is important to practise first.

2 When you have chosen your stitch, place tear-away stabilizer under the first petal and make sure the edges of the petal are opened out flat and not folded under. Begin at the top on the centre crease with the outside right edge of the foot next to the line that is below the raw edge. Sew to the corner, stopping about half the width of the foot away from the crease. If you have one, use the 'Pattern End' or 'Stop' function on your machine. Pivot and continue down the right-hand side of the petal, guiding the foot edge along the creased line (see Fig 9). Secure and remove from the machine.

Begin at the centre top again, with the left edge of the foot on the line below the raw edge. If needed, mirror image the stitch pattern side to side (or take it off if you mirrored it for the first half) and sew the same number of stitch patterns you sewed along the first top half (see page 127 for Mirror Imaging). Pivot at the corner and sew down the other side as before (Fig 10). If you don't have a mirror image function it is easier to select a stitch pattern that is symmetrical. However, if you use an asymmetrical one, begin at the bottom edge and sew to the top

3 For the next row, select a smaller, narrower stitch pattern or adjust the width and length of a larger one. Begin at the lower edge on the crease and sew towards the top edge, lining up the right-hand side of the edge of the foot against the edge of the previous row of stitches. Sew towards the top, stopping about half the width of the foot away from the previous row. Use the 'Pattern End' or 'Stop' function if you have one. Sew along the top, pivot at the corner and then along the next side, keeping the foot edge along the side of the previous stitches (Fig 11).

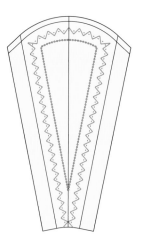

Fig 11

4 For the third row, select a stitch (adjust if necessary) and sew one pattern in the centre at the bottom (Fig 12). Stop with the needle in the fabric, pivot and sew towards the top, lining the foot edge with the edge of the previous stitches and stopping about half a foot width from the second row of stitches (Fig 13). Repeat for the other side (Fig 14). For the top, begin just before the centre crease with the right-hand side of the foot next to the second row of stitches at the top edge. Sew one pattern in the centre and stop (Fig 15). Pivot to adjust the foot to the same angle as the top edge and then sew to the corner (Fig 16).

Turn the petal around and place the needle in the same place you started the centre stitch. Angle the foot so that the left side is next to the second row of stitches and then sew to the corner (Fig 17).

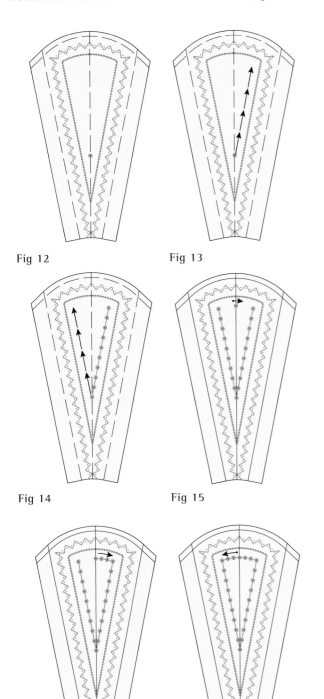

Fig 12

Fig 13

Fig 14

Fig 15

Fig 16

Fig 17

Sewing the Pulled Thread Petals

1 Cut four strips of linen 2in x 8in (5cm x 20.3cm). Read Pulled Thread Sewing on page 114 and follow the steps there to sew a line of pulled thread work down the centre of each linen strip.

2 Pin one strip centrally on each of the four medium shade petals with the rounded tops. Sew the linen to the petals using one of the following three methods:

i) Use a straight stitch scallop on both sides of the linen, lining the edge of the foot up against the edge of the drawn thread work. Trim away the excess linen close to the edge of the stitching (see Fig 18). Sew over the cut edge with a wider satin stitch scallop, stopping after each pattern to make any adjustments. This is the most difficult option and you will have to experiment with stitch lengths and widths in order to make the satin stitch cover the raw edge. The picture below shows the finished effect.

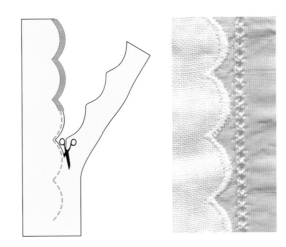

Fig 18

5 Sew the facing, right sides together, to the top edge of each petal using a ¼in (6mm) seam allowance. Do not sew down the sides of the petals. Trim the seam allowances and fold the facing over to the wrong side of the petal. Press the seam edge.

6 Repeat steps 2–5 above for the remaining three decorative petals. Place the petals to one side for the moment.

ii) Sew the linen to the silk using a straight stitch on both sides, lining the edge of the foot against the edge of the drawn thread work. Trim away the excess linen close to the stitching. Select a stitch pattern that will cover the raw edges and sew this on top of the straight stitches (Fig 19). Alternatively, use a regular satin stitch over the straight stitches and then sew a decorative stitch, such as a scallop, at the side (Fig 20). The first picture below shows the finished effect.

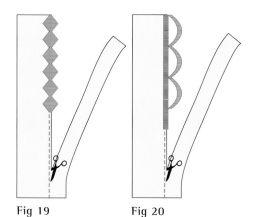

Fig 19   **Fig 20**

iii) Fold the raw edges of the linen to the wrong side, about ¾in (2cm) from the edge of the pulled thread work. Trim the turnings if they show through the holes in the pulled threads. Sew to the background with a decorative stitch such as a straight-edged scallop.

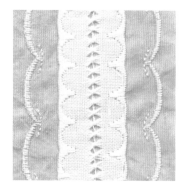

3 Now sew a decorative stitch on the petal either side of the linen. I used an entredeux stitch with a wing needle and guided the edge of the foot along the edge of the scallop on the linen.

4 Sew the facings, right sides together to the top edge of each petal using a ¼in (6mm) seam allowance. Trim the seam and fold the facing over to the wrong side of each petal and press the seam edge.

Sewing the Pointed Petals

1 Sew the facings, right sides together, to the top edge of each of the pointed petals using a ¼in (6mm) seam allowance. Trim the seams and the point and fold the facings over to the wrong side of the petals. Press the seam edge.

2 Using Template 3 on page 28, lightly mark the chain stitching line on each petal. The point at the top of the chain stitching should be ¾in (2cm) from the finished edge at the point of the petal. Use a thread in the top of your machine to match the decorative cord and place tear-away stabilizer underneath the petal. See page 105 for the chain stitching technique.

3 Cut a 15in (38.1cm) length of decorative cord. Beginning at the point at the top of the chain stitching line, sew a chain stitch down the centre. Pull the ends of the cord to the back of the petal using a needle with a large eye.

4 Cut two 7in (17.8cm) lengths of cord. Beginning at the centre vein, sew the two side prongs. Pull the ends of the cord to the back as you did before.

5 Now cut a 28in (71.1cm) length of cord. Sew all around the outside beginning at the bottom of the petal and pivoting at the corners and point (Fig 21). Pull the ends of the cord to the back. The cord ends will be secured when the satin stitch is sewn. Leave the stabilizer in place. Repeat steps 3–5 to sew the other three pointed petals.

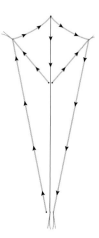

Fig 21

6 Cut four 6in x 3in (15.2cm x 7.6cm) pieces of organza. Place one piece of the organza centrally over each of the petals and machine tack (baste) it in place around the edge of the organza.

tip Take care when using organza and do *not* use a hot iron on the fabric – unless you want it shrivelled!

7 Using an air-erasable marker, draw a line on the organza ¼in (6mm) away from the chain stitching. This will be the guide line for the satin stitching.

8 On each of the petals, zigzag stitch (length 1.0, width 1.0) along the satin stitch line, making sure that the seam allowances at the sides of the petals are opened out before you sew. Trim the organza close to the stitching and then satin stitch over the stitching and the raw edge of the organza (length 0.3, width 2.0). See page 116 for satin stitch appliqué.

9 On each of the petals, sew a candle-wicking or a similar stitch around the outside of the satin stitching, being careful to leave enough space at the sides for the seams. See page 113 for candlewicking. Begin at the top point and sew down to the corner of the base, lining the inside edge of the foot against the edge of the satin stitching. Start again at the top and sew in the other direction ending at the opposite corner of the base. Pivot and sew along the base. By sewing in this way you will ensure that there is a stitch at the top centre point. Carefully remove the stabilizer.

10 To finish each petal, sew a tiny bead at the four points of the chain stitching – I used little pearls.

Sewing the Centre Appliqué

1 For the centre appliqué use an 8in (20.3cm) square of light silk with tear-away stabilizer underneath. If the silk is fine, iron a square of fusible interfacing to the wrong side before beginning. Using different decorative stitches sew circles around the centre, following the steps on page 110 for Circular Sewing. The last circle should measure about 4in (10cm) across the diameter, so your masking tape will need to be at least 2in (5cm) long. The first mark on the tape should be ¾in (2cm) from the needle and then 1in (2.5cm), 1¼in (3.2cm), 1⅝in (4.1cm) and 2in (5cm) from the needle.

2 Draw around the centre appliqué Template 4 on page 29 on the right side of your circular sewing, being careful to place it in the centre.

3 If desired, add one or two decorative stitches in the rounded and pointed areas between the last row of circular sewing and the line around the outside of the shape (see photo above).

Making Up the Block

1 Trim off the top edge of each of the rounded and pointed petal templates along the dotted line. This will result in a template of the finished size of each petal. Place the template on the wrong side of the finished silk petal, with the finished top edge of the silk petal even with the top edge of the template and in the centre, and with an equal distance from the edge of the last row of stitching at each side. This will be much easier to judge if you cut the template out of template plastic as you will be able to see through it. Draw a line on the silk ¼in (6mm) away from the template sides and cut the silk petal on the line. Do *not* cut next to the template because you will need ¼in (6mm) seam allowances at the sides.

2 Lay the petals on a flat surface in the order of the finished design (see picture on page 16). With right sides facing, pin the petals together. Starting at the top edges where the facings are, sew the petals together using a ¼in (6mm) seam allowance. Press seams open.

3 Crease the calico background along the diagonals and in half along each side. Pin the sewn petals centrally on the calico, using the creases as a guide.

4 Pin and/or tack (baste) a square of wadding (batting) underneath the background. Stitch in the seam ditches (see tip below) between the petals (stitch length 3.0).

5 Using a buttonhole appliqué stitch or similar and a walking foot, sew around the outside edge of the petals. Refer to the finished-edge appliqué technique on page 114.

6 Remove the stabilizer from the back of the circular sewn centre. Iron the square of fusible web to the back of the centre piece and cut out the shape on the marked line. Peel off the backing paper. Place the centre design in the middle of the petals with the points at the edge of the design over the centre of the base of the pointed petals. Press in place using a pressing sheet to prevent any marks from the iron. With a piece of tear-away stabilizer underneath, appliqué the centre to the petals around the edge using a satin stitch of width 2.5. See page 116 for Satin Stitch Appliqué.

7 Sew a candlewicking stitch or other small decorative stitch pattern around the outside of the Dresden Plate block, lining up the edge of the foot with the edge of the petals. Remove the tear-away stabilizer and sew a bead in the centre and at the edge of the centre design where the rounded edges meet the pointed edges. Sew a bead at the top of each seam that joins the petals. Cut the block to 21in (53.3cm) square – this includes ½in (1.3mm) seam allowances. Your centre block is now finished: for the next block see page 30.

tip

Sewing (or quilting) in the ditch means stitching in the seam line (or sometimes very close to it). The stitches are not only hidden in the seam but stabilize the quilt top and wadding (batting).

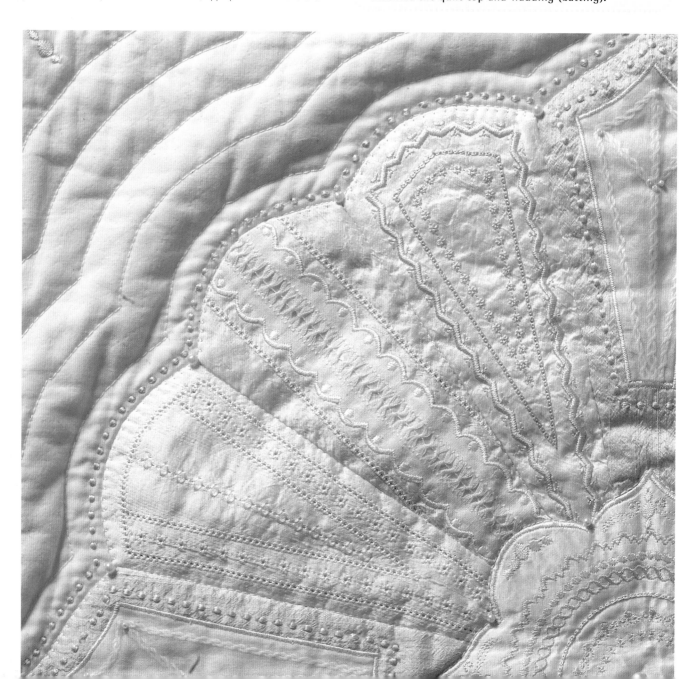

The decorative stitching seen in the Dresden Plate
block can be used to embellish all sorts of items.
Here, the collar and neck details on some simple
silk pyjamas are decorated with delicate machine
stitching. Try the effect on a nightdress or bed linen.

Nine-Patch Cushion

This pretty cushion is made from two shades of silk but you could make it from a fabric of your choice, perhaps a tone-on-tone quilting cotton or two shades of linen. The colour difference could be subtle or dramatically different. All of the techniques on this cushion, apart from the binding and triple stitching, are ones you will have used in the Dresden Plate block. The corner squares are cut from a large square of circular sewing, which means you don't have to match up the stitch patterns at the beginning and end of each circle because the joins are hidden in the seam allowance. I am lucky in that I have lots of pretty stitches on my machine, but if you don't have much of a selection, simply repeat the ones you do have – they will look fine when sewn in a circle.

you will need

- Fabric A: ¼yd (0.25m) x 45in (115cm) wide for decorative sides
- Fabric B: 1yd (1m) x 45in (115cm) wide for corners, centre, binding and backs
- Thin cord or six-stranded embroidery thread for corded sewing 2yd (2m) approximately
- Wadding (batting) one 19in (48.3cm) square and one 7½in (19cm)
- Calico or similar, to back cushion front one 19in (48.3cm) square
- Tear-away stabilizer
- Rayon machine embroidery thread to match each of the fabrics
- Machine sewing thread (polyester or cotton) to match fabric B
- Machine needle size 60 or 70 and a wing needle
- Masking tape
- Air-erasable fabric marker
- Cushion pad 18in x 18in (46cm x 46cm)
- Drawing pin, masking tape and electrical tape
- Light box (optional)

Finished size of cushion: 18in x 18in (46cm x 46cm)
Techniques: wing needle sewing (page 112) • decorative stitching (page 106) • chain stitching (page 105) • triple stitch (page 109) candlewicking by machine (page 113) • circular sewing (page 110) double-fold binding with mitred corners (page 141)

Preparing the Fabric

1 From Fabric B, cut a 14in (35.5cm) square. Fold in half in both directions and open to find the centre. Draw a line with an air-erasable marker from the centre along a crease to the edge. This will be where you begin and end each line of stitching for the circular sewing.

2 Thread your machine with the rayon thread that matches Fabric A on the top and machine sewing thread in a similar colour to the fabric or the top thread in the bobbin. Stick a strip of masking tape to the right of the needle, lining up the top of the tape with the needle. Beginning 1in (2.5cm) away from the needle, mark every ⅜in (1cm) for quite close lines of stitching or every ½in (1.3cm) for lines a little further apart. Secure a drawing pin, point up, at the first mark (see picture, right, and page 110 for instructions on Circular Sewing).

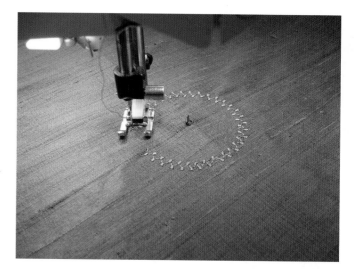

Circular Sewing

3 Place the centre of the square (with the stabilizer underneath) over the drawing pin. Select a stitch pattern and begin with the needle on the marked line. Sew the circle and end on the line (see picture right). Don't worry about matching up the pattern design at the end as this part will be hidden in the seam allowance. Move the pin to the next mark and continue sewing circles of stitch patterns to fill the square. If the hole is getting a little large, iron on two small squares of fusible stabilizer on top of each other on the back, over the hole.

4 Leaving the stabilizer on the back, cut the square to 13in (33cm) and then cut it into four squares, each measuring 6½in (16.5cm).

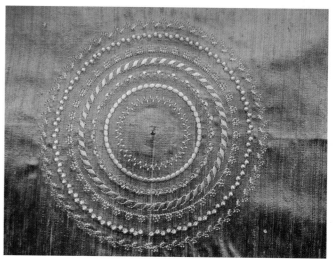

Decorative Sewing

5 From Fabric A, cut out four 7½in (19cm) squares and place tear-away stabilizer underneath. Decorate with lines of wing needle sewing (see page 112 Wing Needle Sewing), decorative stitch patterns (see page 106 Decorative Stitching) and chain stitching (see page 105 Chain Stitching). Begin by marking the centre line of stitching and then sewing lines to each side, guiding the edge of the foot against the previous line of stitching. Use rayon thread to match the fabric for the wing needle sewing, one that matches Fabric B for the decorative stitches and a thread to match the cord or embroidery thread for the chain stitching. Sew the lines to within 1in (2.5cm) from the raw edges at the sides. Either leave the stabilizer on or remove it depending on the weight of your fabric – I left it on as the silk was quite flimsy. Trim each square to 6½in (16.5cm).

6 Cut one 7½in (19cm) square from fabric B and using the cushion Template 1 on page 29, draw the centre pattern on the right side. If you don't have a light box to draw the pattern, hold it up to a window to see through the fabric. If you still can't see through, then trace the design on to tissue paper or special quilting paper and pin this to the right side of the fabric. Stitch through the paper and tear it away after the design has been sewn.

7 Place a square of wadding underneath and then tear-away stabilizer under the wadding. Stitch around the design with a triple stitch (see page 109 Triple Stitch), a candlewicking stitch (see page 113 Candlewicking by Machine) or similar small pattern. At the base of each petal, sew one stitch pattern (use the 'Pattern End' or 'Stop' function on your machine if applicable) sewing from the base towards the centre of the petal. Secure the thread at the beginning by either using the 'fix' function or by sewing a few straight stitches, length 0. If your pattern is a satin-stitched design, bring the thread tail in front of the needle and sew the first few stitches of the pattern over it. Cut the thread off and continue sewing the stitch pattern, trapping the end of the thread. This way you won't have to pull the thread tail to the back.

8 Sew a stitch pattern at each of the petal points in a similar way (see example in picture, top right). Remove the stabilizer and cut the square to 6½in (16.5cm). Trim the wadding ½in (1.3cm) from each raw edge.

Piecing the Cushion Front

9 Sew the squares together in three rows with a ⅜in (1cm) seam. Draw two parallel lines ⅜in (1cm) apart on a scrap of paper. Place this under the presser foot with the line at the right on the edge of the foot. Move your needle over so that it lines up with the line on the left. When you sew the seam, line up the edge of the fabric with the edge of the foot and the needle will be in the correct position to sew a ⅜in (1cm) seam. Trim off the stabilizer in the seam allowance of the decorative squares and press the seams open. Sew the three rows together matching the seams (Fig 1) – see also the Tip below.

Fig 1

tip

When sewing the seam, pin where the seams meet and sew this small section, beginning about ½in (1.3cm) before and ending ½in (1.3cm) after the seams meet. Check they match – if they are out of line you only have to undo this small section rather than the whole seam. When you are happy with the alignment, sew the entire seam. There's no need to remove this first section of stitches, just sew over them.

Making Up the Cushion

10 Pin a 19in (48.3cm) square of wadding (batting) beneath the cushion top and a 19in (48.3cm) square of calico beneath the wadding. Quilt in the ditch of the seams with a straight stitch. Trim the wadding and backing to the same size as the cushion front.

11 Cut two rectangles from Fabric B each 19in x 13in (48.3cm x 33cm). Make the pieces for the cushion back by turning under a ½in (1.3cm) double hem to the wrong side on one long edge of each back piece. Machine the two hems near the edge (Fig 2). Place the back pieces on your work surface, wrong sides up and overlap them until they are the same width as the cushion front. Pin the cushion front on top, right side up, and trim the lengths of the backs level with the edges of the top. Pin and, using a walking foot, sew around the edge with a long straight stitch about ¼in (6mm) from the raw edges (Fig 3). This is to tack (baste) all the layers together to make binding easier. Because it is only ¼in (6mm) from the edge, it will be within the binding and won't show, so you don't have to remove it. Line up the edge of the walking foot with the edge of the fabric and move the needle over so it is about ¼in (6mm) away from the edge. This means that all of the foot is on the fabric rather than hanging over the edge and causing problems.

12 For the binding, cut a strip or strips from Fabric B measuring 2½in (6.3cm) wide by a total length of about 80in (203cm). Join the strips with a diagonal seam (see step 3, page 141) and fold wrong sides together in half, lengthways. Bind the cushion using a walking foot and a ⅜in (1cm) seam (see page 141 Double-Fold Binding with Mitred Corners). Insert the cushion pad to finish.

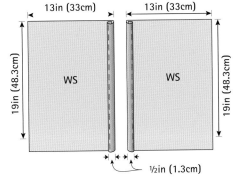

Fig 2

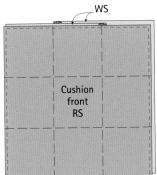

Fig 3

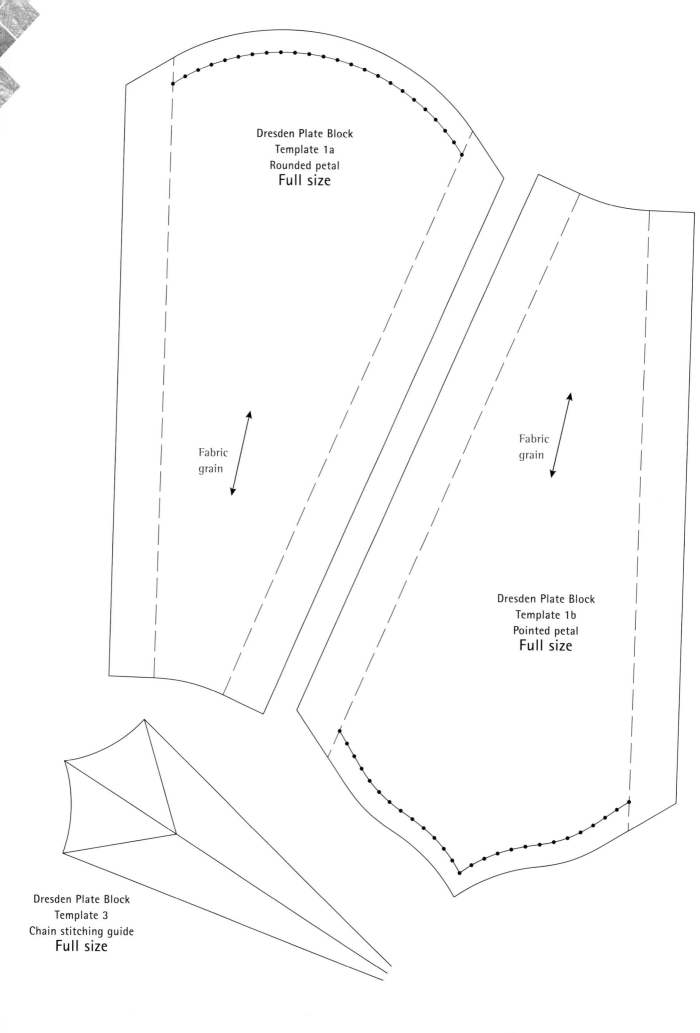

Dresden Plate Block
Template 1a
Rounded petal
Full size

Fabric
grain

Fabric
grain

Dresden Plate Block
Template 1b
Pointed petal
Full size

Dresden Plate Block
Template 3
Chain stitching guide
Full size

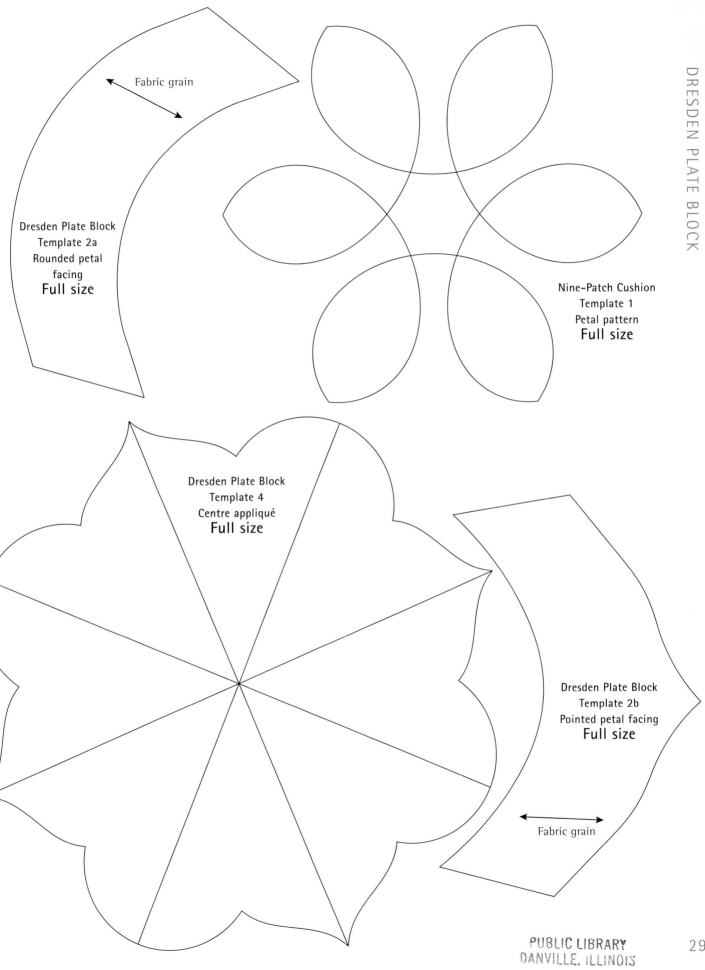

Fabric grain

Dresden Plate Block
Template 2a
Rounded petal
facing
Full size

Nine-Patch Cushion
Template 1
Petal pattern
Full size

Dresden Plate Block
Template 4
Centre appliqué
Full size

Dresden Plate Block
Template 2b
Pointed petal facing
Full size

Fabric grain

Shadow Appliqué Block

Shadow appliqué uses transparent fabrics to create a soft and delicate effect. A top layer of transparent fabric is marked with an appliqué pattern and stitched to a lower layer of fabric, which is then trimmed away outside these stitches. The templates required are given full size on pages 34–35. There are two Shadow Appliqué blocks in the Heirloom Quilt. The instructions in this section are for making one of them.

Finished size of block: 15⅛in x 15⅛in (38.4cm x 38.4cm) includes ½in (1.3cm) seam allowance for quilt assembly

Techniques: satin stitch appliqué (page 116) • shadow appliqué (page 118) • chain stitching (page 105) • lace shaping (page 119) echo quilting (page 133) • finished-edge appliqué (page 114)

Preparing the Appliqués

1 Fold the background square in half diagonally and iron to make a crease. Open out and fold the other way diagonally and make another crease.

2 Trace around the large shell shape Template 1 on page 34 four times on the paper side of the fusible web and roughly cut out each shell shape outside the drawn line (Fig 1). Place the shapes, sticky side down on the wrong side of the dark shade of silk (Fig 2). Make sure they will all fit before you fuse them in place. Cut out each shell shape on the drawn line.

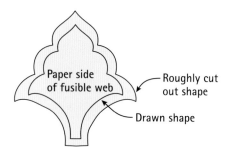

Paper side of fusible web — Roughly cut out shape — Drawn shape

Fig 1

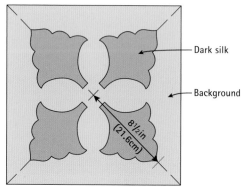

Cut on line after fusing (there will be four of these shapes) — Wrong side of dark silk — Paper side of fusible web

Fig 2

you will need

(to make two blocks multiply the amounts given by two)
- Calico or chosen background fabric 18in (45.7cm) square
- Dark shade silk of ¼yd (0.25m) x 45in (115cm)
- Light shade of silk 10in x 6in (25.4cm x 15.2cm)
- Medium shade of silk 6in (15.2cm) square
- Organza 7in x 25in (17.8cm x 63.5cm)
- Edging lace ½in (1.3cm) wide x 1¼yd (1.25m)
- Fine decorative cord 3yd (3m) approximately
- Wadding (batting) 18in (45.7cm) square
- Fusible web, e.g., Bondaweb (Wonder Under) or Steam-A-Seam 2, one piece 18in x 12in (45.7cm x 30.5cm) and one 5in x 12in (12.7cm x 30.5cm)
- Tear-away stabilizer
- Threads: rayon machine embroidery thread 40 weight to match dark silk shade; 40 weight to match light silk shade and machine thread for the bobbin and to match the lace
- One bead (5mm–6mm diameter)
- Machine needle size 60 or 70
- Open-toe foot

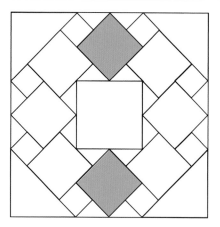

Position of the two Shadow Appliqué Blocks in the Heirloom Quilt

3 Peel off the paper backing from the fusible web and place the shells centrally over the creases on the background fabric, with the tip at the top of each shell 8½in (21.6cm) from the centre. Check to make sure that opposite tips are 17in (43.2cm) apart and that the base of each shell is centred over the crease. Press carefully to fuse in place (Fig 3).

Dark silk — Background — 8½in (21.6cm)

Fig 3

4 Thread your machine with rayon 40 weight thread to match or coordinate with the silk you are using for the appliqué, and either cotton, polyester or bobbin thread in the bobbin. Use an open-toe foot and satin stitch (width 3.0) around the edge of each shell (see page 116 Satin Stitch Appliqué). Begin at the bottom corner, sew all the way around and end at the other bottom corner. There is no need to satin stitch the base as this will be covered by the centre appliqué.

tip

When deciding which thread you prefer in the bobbin, sew a sample of satin stitch. There shouldn't be any of the bobbin thread showing on the top, but some of the top thread should be pulling through to the underside. The stitch should have a rounded effect on the top and be quite flat underneath. Adjust the bobbin thread and/or tension to achieve a good-looking stitch.

5 Using the smaller shell shape for the organza shape, Template 2 on page 34, draw around the outside of it on to the large shells you have satin stitched (Fig 4). You could cut the shape out from template plastic first and then draw around that. Use an easily removable or light-coloured marker. The tip of the small shell should be 1¾in (4.4cm) from the tip of the large shell.

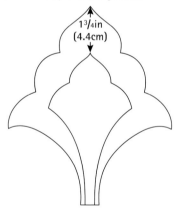

1¾in (4.4cm)

Fig 4

6 For the next step, you could use either Steam-A-Seam 2, which has a fusible web sandwiched between two sheets of backing paper, or Bondaweb (Wonder Under) which has just one sheet of backing paper. If using Steam-A-Seam 2, first peel off one side of backing paper at a corner to test which paper the web is stuck to. This will be the side you draw on. For Bondaweb (Wonder Under), draw on the paper side. Draw around four of each of the appliqué for shells light shade Template 3a and 3b and one of the appliqué for centre light shade Template 4a and 4b on page 35. Cut around the shapes leaving a small border. If using Steam-A-Seam 2, peel off the backing paper leaving the web still attached to the backing paper that has the drawing. Press the shapes on the wrong side of the light silk, sticky-side down and cut them out on the drawn line. Repeat for the medium shade using Templates 5a and 5b and 6a and 6b.

7 Place the appliqué shapes for the centre (4a, 4b, 6a and 6b) to one side for later. Carefully position and fuse the remaining shapes on to the large shells that have been satin stitched to the background, following Fig 5 and Fig 6 for placements.

Fig 5

Adding the Organza

8 Cut out four rectangles from organza, each measuring about 7in x 5in (17.8cm x 12.7cm). Place one of these centrally over each large shell, making sure it overlaps the outline of the small shell shape drawn on the background earlier. Tack (baste) in place around the edge. Now follow the instructions for Shadow Appliqué on page 118, in particular step 3.

9 You should be able to see the line marking the outline of the small shell shape through the organza. If this is a little difficult to see, either draw around it again on the organza or use the template and re-mark. Using the same thread you used for the satin stitching, zigzag stitch (length 1.0, width 0.5) on the drawn line. Trim away the organza from the outside close to the stitching (Fig 6).

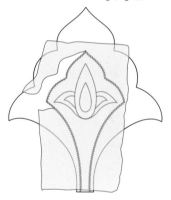

Fig 6

10 Now choose a satin stitch design to sew around the zigzagged raw edge of the organza. I used a small satin circle but you could use a different one or a narrow satin stitch.

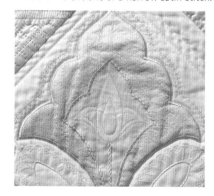

11 Using decorative cord, sew a chain stitch (see page 105) in the centre below the appliqué to represent the stem.

Creating the Lace Shaping

12 For the lace shaping that is between the shells, draw around the oval Template 7 four times on a piece of calico. The lace ovals will be shaped on this calico before placing them on to the background. Beginning at the bottom of the oval, leave a ½in (1.3cm) tail and shape a length of edging lace along the drawn line (see page 119 Lace Shaping). There's no need to finish off the base of the oval with a mitre as this will be covered by the centre shape. When the lace ovals are shaped, pin them to the background in the gaps between the large shells. Using a thread to match the lace, straight stitch around the inner oval and use a narrow zigzag stitch around the outside of the oval.

13 Pin and tack (baste) the wadding (batting) to the wrong side of the square. Using a narrow zigzag stitch, couch a length of cord (see page 111) on the inside edge of the pulled lace. Begin at the bottom of the lace and leave a short tail of cord at the beginning and end. This will be hidden under the centre shape.

14 Sew a decorative stitch around the outside of the large shells, lining up the edge of the presser foot with the edge of the shell (see page 133 Echo Quilting). I used a small star/flower shape, but choose one of your own or use a candlewicking stitch (see page 113).

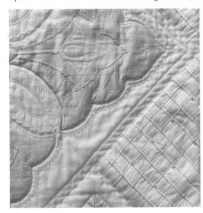

Finishing the Centre

15 For the centre, draw around the centre Template 8 on to a 5in (12.7cm) square of tear-away stabilizer. Iron fusible interfacing to the wrong side of a 5in (12.7cm) square of dark silk. Pin the stabilizer, drawn side up on to the interfaced side of the silk and straight stitch on the drawn line to mark the outline of the centre shape (Fig 7). Cut a 5in (13cm) square of organza and, using the appliqué shapes you set aside earlier and the organza square, shadow appliqué them (see page 118) to the centre in layered order 4b, 6b, 4a and 6a. Sew a straight stitch for each accent line at the base of the large scallop top petals (see picture detail with step 17). Trim or tear away the stabilizer on the wrong side of the silk around the outside of the stitching/marked line.

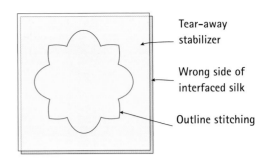

Tear-away stabilizer

Wrong side of interfaced silk

Outline stitching

Fig 7

16 For the facing, cut a 5in (12.7cm) square of dark silk and pin this to the centre square over the organza, right sides together. With the wrong side of the shadow appliqué on top, sew around the outline stitching (Fig 8). Trim about ⅛in (3mm) from the stitching and clip the seam allowances at the inside curves (Fig 9). Make a slit in the centre of the facing fabric and turn through to the right side. Use a point turner around the inside edge of the shape to make sure the seam is right on the edge and then press. Be very careful when pressing organza – *don't* use a hot iron otherwise all your lovely work might shrivel up!

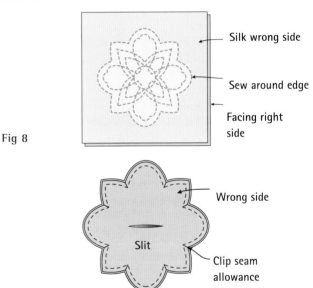

Silk wrong side

Sew around edge

Facing right side

Fig 8

Wrong side

Slit

Clip seam allowance

Fig 9

17 Appliqué the finished shape to the centre of the block (see page 114 Finished-Edge Appliqué). Sew a bead in the centre. Your shadow appliqué block is finished: for the next block see page 36.

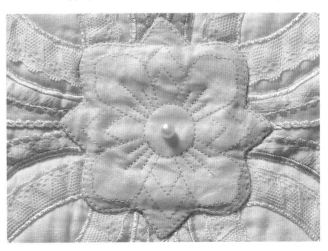

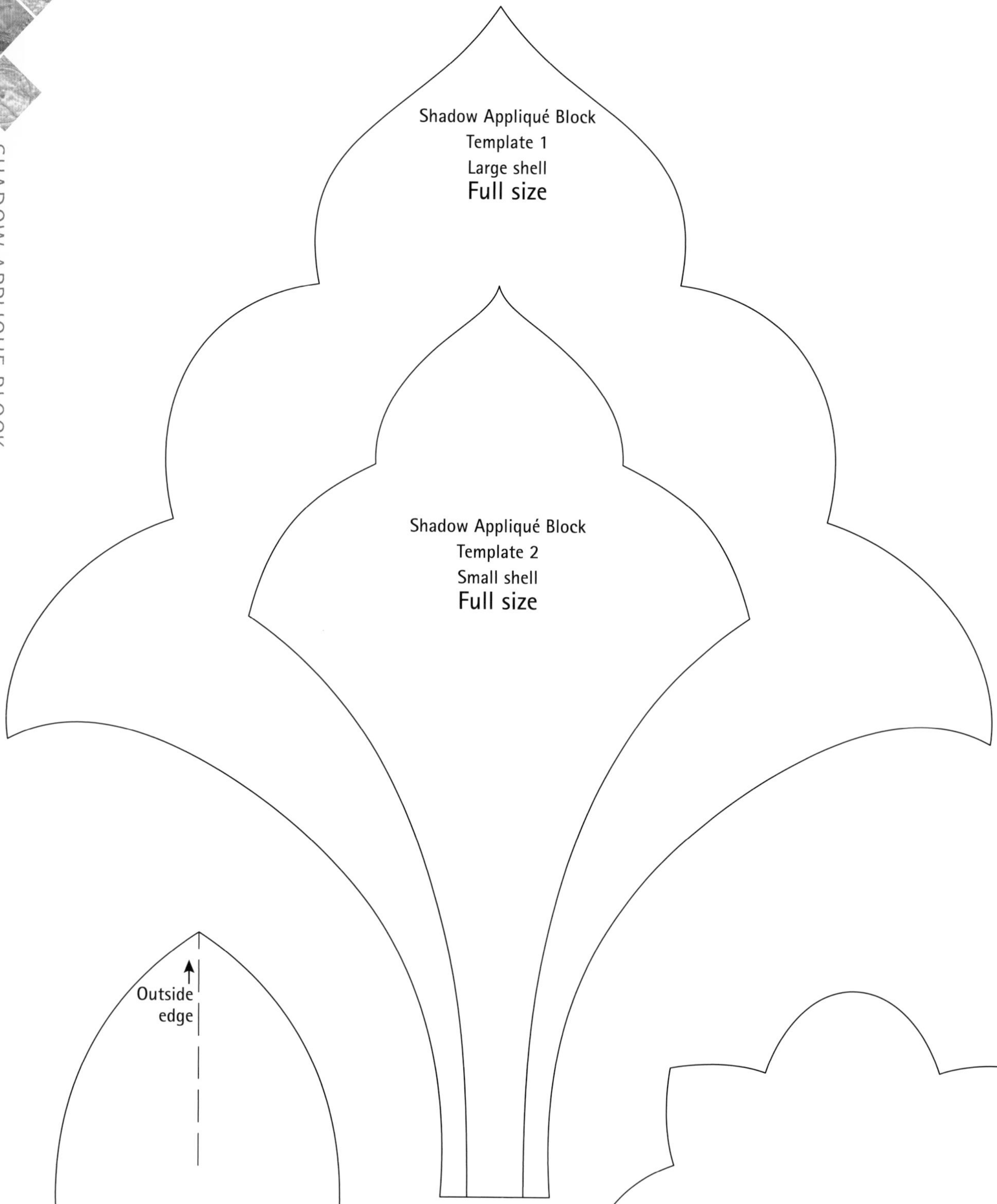

Shadow Appliqué Block
Template 1
Large shell
Full size

Shadow Appliqué Block
Template 2
Small shell
Full size

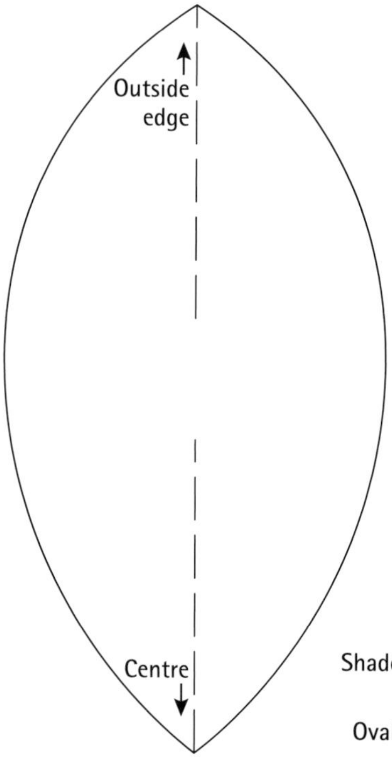

Outside
edge

Centre

Shadow Appliqué Block
Template 7
Oval for lace shaping
Full size

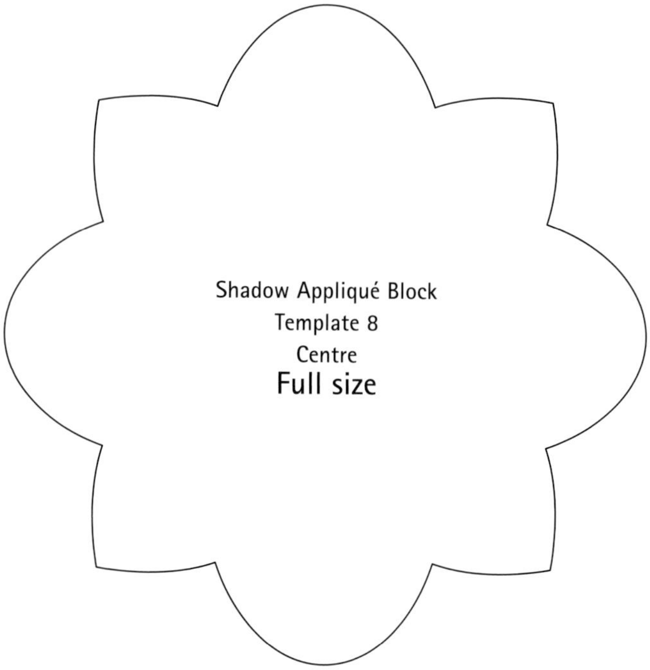

Shadow Appliqué Block
Template 8
Centre
Full size

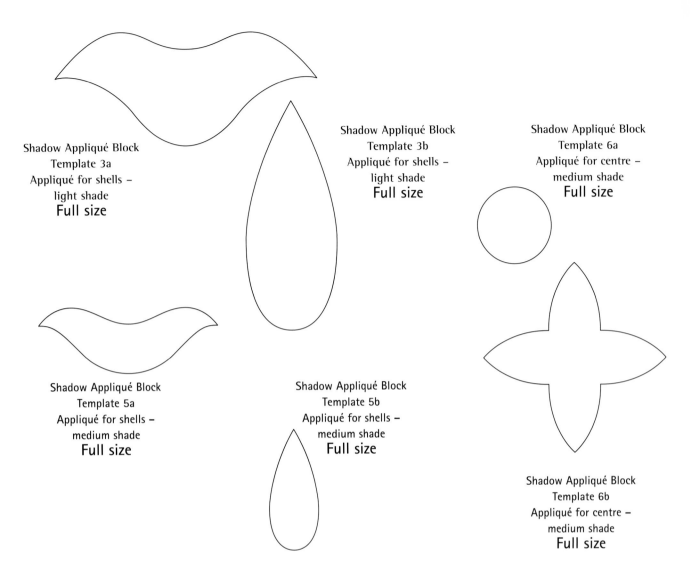

Shadow Appliqué Block
Template 3a
Appliqué for shells –
light shade
Full size

Shadow Appliqué Block
Template 3b
Appliqué for shells –
light shade
Full size

Shadow Appliqué Block
Template 6a
Appliqué for centre –
medium shade
Full size

Shadow Appliqué Block
Template 5a
Appliqué for shells –
medium shade
Full size

Shadow Appliqué Block
Template 5b
Appliqué for shells –
medium shade
Full size

Shadow Appliqué Block
Template 6b
Appliqué for centre –
medium shade
Full size

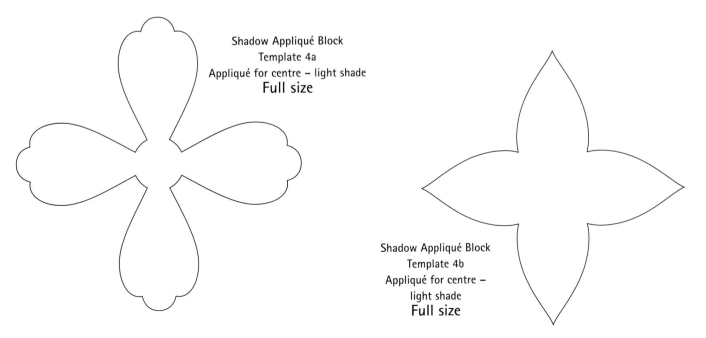

Shadow Appliqué Block
Template 4a
Appliqué for centre – light shade
Full size

Shadow Appliqué Block
Template 4b
Appliqué for centre –
light shade
Full size

Puffing Block

The four Puffing blocks in the Heirloom Quilt include lots of beautiful techniques that you would find on handmade antique Christening gowns and you will be surprised at how easy they are to sew on your machine. Templates are given full size on pages 46–47. The directions and requirements in the materials list are for making one block. Economical calico is suggested because there is so much decorative sewing on these blocks that very little of the original fabric will show. An elegant roll pillow on page 43 is the perfect project to try some of the techniques before you start the quilt block.

Finished size of block: 15⅛in x 15⅛in (38.4cm x 38.4cm), includes ½in (1.3cm) seam allowance for quilt assembly
Techniques: puffing (page 124) • faggoting (page 126) • mirror imaging (page 127) • sewing over cord (page 109) • corded entredeux (page 128) • continuous sewing (page 105) • twin needle pin-tucks (page 129) • double-fold binding with mitred corners (page 141)

Joining Pieces A and B

Each Puffing block is made up of four puffing strips and eight triangles, and each triangle is composed of piece A and piece B. Pieces A and B are decorated with rows of machine stitching but because stitch widths vary on different makes and models of machines, from 5mm to 9mm, giving specific distances between the rows is difficult. However, it's all very flexible and as long as each piece is sewn with exactly the same distances as each other, it will all fit together. It is a good idea to sew one section as a practice piece before you sew the real thing. Template 1 is given on page 46 as a guide so that you are able to judge the size of the finished section, but don't worry if yours isn't exactly the same – as long as they are the same as each other. The pattern pieces are larger than needed as the shape will be trimmed to the correct size after all the stitching has been completed.

1 From the calico or silk cut out eight of piece A from Template 2 on page 47 and eight of piece B from Template 3, making sure that you cut four of each with the pattern face *up* and four with the pattern face *down*. You may want to cut one additional set of both shapes for practice, or to use as a spare if needed.

2 On the wrong side of shapes A and B mark a line 1in (2.5cm) from edge C (see Fig 1). Fold and press the raw edge to the line on each piece. This will give you a ½in (1.3cm) turning. You should have four of each piece facing one way and four facing the other way.

you will need
(to make four blocks multiply the amounts given by four)
- Calico 18in (46cm) square
- Wadding (batting) 18in (46cm) square
- Calico or silk (medium shade) ⅓yd x 45in (0.3m x 115cm)
- Silk (light shade) or fine cotton such as batiste for puffing strips, four strips 2in (5cm) wide x 24in (61cm) long (cut strip lengths parallel to selvedge if using silk but perpendicular if using fine cotton, testing both grains beforehand to see which gathers best)
- Silk (light shade) for 'tulips' 4in (10cm) square
- Silk (medium shade) for 'tulips' 4in (10cm) square
- Silk (dark shade) for centre square 5in (12.5cm) square
- Fusible interfacing 5in (12.5cm) square
- Silk (dark shade) for outer edge 1in (2.5cm) wide x 1½yd (1.5m) long – shorter lengths can be joined
- Organza or dark silk for behind faggoting, eight strips 1in x 7in (2.5cm x 18cm)
- Ribbon for inner square edge ¼in (6mm) wide x ½yd (0.5m)
- Ribbon ³⁄₁₆in or ¼in (5mm or 6mm) wide x 1yd (1m) – choose a width the same or less than maximum width of decorative stitches
- Fine decorative cord for faggoting 1yd (1m) (optional – see Suppliers)
- Decorative stranded cord 6yd (5m) (see Suppliers)
- Fine cord such as crochet cotton for twin needle pin-tucks 3½yd (3.25m) (optional)
- Perlé no.8 thread or crochet cotton for corded entredeux 6yd (5m) (optional)
- One bead (5mm–6mm diameter)
- Threads: 40 weight rayon machine embroidery to match dark silk shade; 40 weight rayon machine embroidery to match light silk shade; machine thread for the bobbin; machine thread to match lace
- Needles: machine needle size 60 or 70; a twin needle 2.0mm and a wing needle
- Open-toe foot
- Tear-away stabilizer
- Bias tape maker ½in (1.3cm) (optional)
- Optional accessory feet: gathering foot, Spanish hemstitching foot or guide, five-groove pin-tucking foot, seven-hole or three-groove cording foot and a walking foot (see page 104)

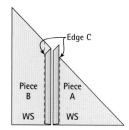

Fig 1

Position of the four Puffing blocks in the Heirloom Quilt

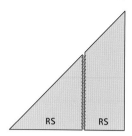

3 Refer to Faggoting on page 126 and join each piece A to each piece B along folded edge C with a faggoting stitch (Fig 2).

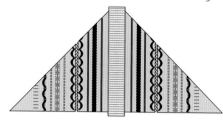

Fig 2

4 To keep the gap at the faggoting open, place a 1in (2.5cm) wide strip of organza or contrasting shade of silk behind the faggoting and sew a scallop stitch or similar either side, guiding the inside edge of the presser foot along the folded edge next to the faggoting. Use tear-away stabilizer underneath. You will need to mirror image your stitch design for one side of the faggoting (see page 127 Mirror Imaging). Tear off the stabilizer and trim the raw edges on the wrong side next to the scallop stitching.

tip If your sewing machine does not have a mirror imaging function, then turn the piece of work around and sew from the bottom to the top.

Decorating Piece B

5 On piece B, refer to Template 1 and mark a line where the corded stitches will be sewn. It is easier to keep the row of stitching straight if the line is marked where the edge of the cords will be, so you don't cover the line as you sew. Place tear-away stabilizer underneath and sew a decorative stitch over two or three strands of decorative cord (see page 109 Sewing over Cord). Tear off the stabilizer and replace it for the next row of stitching.

6 Refer to theCorded Entredeux technique on page 128 and sew a line either side of the corded stitches. Ideally, the corded entredeux should be halfway between the scallop stitches and the corded stitches on one side and the same distance from the corded stitches on the other side. To avoid having short lengths of cut cord at the end of each piece, continue sewing the next piece without cutting the threads (see page 105 Continuous Sewing). If you are unable to sew this stitch on your machine, any wing needle stitch without cord would work well. Check that you are still on track using the template as a guide.

7 Trim the raw edge on piece B 2⅜in (6cm) away from the centre of the faggoting. There will only be a little to trim off.

Making and Inserting the Puffing

8 For the puffing strips, gather each strip down both long sides so that the finished length measures at least 8in (20.3cm). Refer to the puffing technique on page 124.

9 Sew the puffing strips, between two opposite piece B shapes, placing right sides together and sewing a ½in (1.2cm) seam (Fig 3). Trim the puffing seam allowances to about half their original width.

Fig 3

Decorating Piece A

10 On piece A, mark two lines about the same distance from the faggoting as the entredeux lines are on piece B. Sew a row of twin needle pin-tucks on both lines (see page 129 Twin Needle Pin-tucks). Sew a decorative stitch between the two rows of twin needle pin-tucks. See Template 1 for guidance.

11 Use a ribbon that is the same width or narrower than the maximum stitch width on your machine and choose a decorative stitch to sew over it. A symmetrical, open one would look best, such as a cross stitch, star or stretch zigzag. Refer to the stitching guide for the placement and use tear-away stabilizer beneath. Sew another decorative stitch between the ribbon and the shorter row of twin needle stitching.

Joining the Triangles

12 Cut all the shapes to the size of a 10in (25.5cm) square cut in half diagonally (size includes seam allowances). The best way to do this is to cut the triangle out of template plastic first and then draw round it on your pieces before cutting.

13 Sew the pieces together in pairs as in Fig 4 with a ½in (1.3cm) seam allowance, matching the rows of decorative sewing as closely as possible. Don't worry too much about the centre as this will be covered by the centre square. I suggest that you sew them together initially using a larger stitch length as you may need to adjust them slightly in order for the rows to line up. Using a walking foot will help to keep the pieces on top of one another.

Fig 4

14 Press the seams open and then sew the two pairs together to form a square. Press the seams open.

Making the Centre Square

15 Iron fusible interfacing on the back of the 5in (12.7cm) square of the dark shade of silk and cut it into four 2½in (6.3cm) squares. Cut the medium and light shade squares each into four 2in (5cm) squares.

16 To make each 'tulip', place a light-coloured square on top of a medium-coloured square, right sides together, and sew across the diagonal. Cut the two fabrics ¼in (6mm) away from the seam line on one side only and discard the two smaller triangles (Fig 5). Press the seam open and then fold along the seam, wrong sides together and iron flat. Repeat for the remaining squares of light and medium silk.

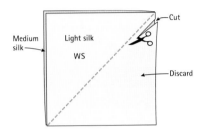

Fig 5

17 Open out each square and fold in half the opposite way. Finger press the light silk only along the fold (Fig 6). Open out and fold in half again, wrong sides together, along the seam (Fig 7). With the light shade uppermost and the seam at the top, pinch the bottom corner of the light silk only (point A on Fig 7) and bring it to the right corner (point B).

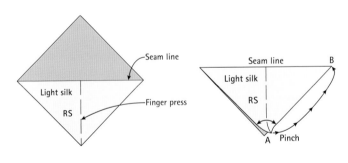

Fig 6   **Fig 7**

18 Now pinch the top fabric at the new bottom corner (at point C at the end of the seam line) and bring it to the right corner (point B) (Fig 8). Pin and hand tack (baste) along the raw edges (Fig 9). Repeat for the remaining three light and medium squares.

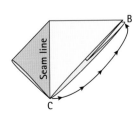   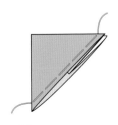

Fig 8   **Fig 9**

19 Mark a dot on the front of one square of dark silk in the top left-hand corner, ¼in (6mm) in from the top and side edges. Pin a tulip, matching raw edges, to the top of the square with the point of the thin end of the tulip (which has only one fold along the edge) at the marked corner of the square. Place it so that the folded edge of the tulip is right next to the dot and tack in place (Fig 10). Pin another square of dark silk on top with right sides facing. Make sure the grain line on both of the squares is running in the same direction. Sew a ¼in (6mm) seam along the raw edges (Fig 11).

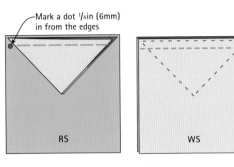

Fig 10   **Fig 11**

20 Repeat step 19 for the two remaining dark silk squares and one of the tulips. Iron the seams open on both pieces so that the tulips lie flat and centred on the front. It is very important that the tulips lie centrally.

21 Place one of the pieces right side up, with the point of the tulip that is sewn into the seam at the top. Place the two remaining tulips at the top edge with the ends that have one fold overlapping in the centre. The folds at the sides of the tulips should cross at the point of the tulip that is sewn into the seam. Pin and tack (baste) in place (Fig 12).

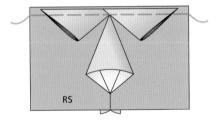

Fig 12

22 Pin the remaining rectangle that has the other tulip sewn into the seam on top with right sides facing, matching centre seams. Tack (baste) and sew ¼in (6mm) from the raw edges (Fig 13). Press the seams open and trim the square to 4in (10cm). Sew a bead in the centre.

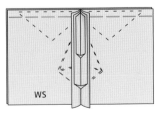

Fig 13

Finishing the Block

23 Trim the puffing square to 12½in (31.7cm). Pin this in the centre of the 18in (45.7cm) square of calico and tack (baste) the wadding (batting) to the back. Stitch in the seam ditches of the diagonal seams. Use the buttonhole appliqué stitch or straight stitch either side of the puffing strips.

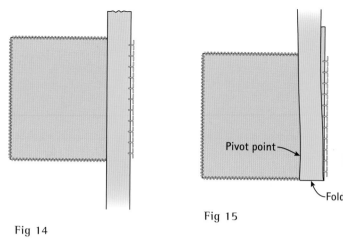

Fig 14

Fig 15

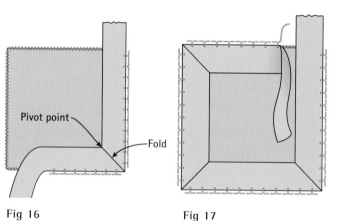

Fig 16

Fig 17

24 Pin the tulip square diagonally over the centre. Using a walking foot, zigzag stitch (length 3.5, width 3.5) over the raw edges of the tulip square and the outside raw edges of the puffing square, going through all thicknesses.

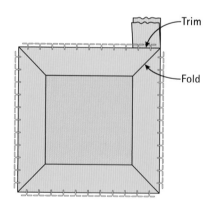

Fig 18

25 Starting at a corner, sew the narrow ribbon over the zigzagged edges of the tulip square. Sew the outside edge of the ribbon first, leaving a 1in (2.5cm) tail at the beginning (Fig 14). Use a buttonhole appliqué stitch or similar. If your machine doesn't have this stitch you could use a small zigzag stitch or blind hem stitch adjusted shorter and narrower than the default setting – see Finished-Edge Appliqué page 115, step 3. Fix the stitch at the first corner, making sure the stitch doesn't sew into the ribbon too near to the corner – move the ribbon out of the way if necessary. Take the fabric out of the machine, fold the ribbon back on itself (Fig 15) and then down, parallel to the next side, forming a mitre (Fig 16). Repeat for the next two corners. Stop sewing when you are close to the beginning and remove the fabric from the machine (Fig 17). Fold under the end of the ribbon forming a mitre at the last corner. Pin and sew to the corner. Trim the ribbon end close to stitching (Fig 18). Using the same stitch, sew down the inside edge of the ribbon (Fig 19).

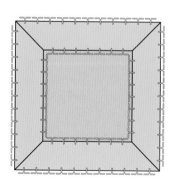

Fig 19

26 To make the strip that is sewn around the edge of the puffing square, cut 1in (2.5cm) strips of silk preferably on the straight grain (parallel to the selvedge) as this will result in less fraying. You will need approximately 1½yd (1.4m) but you can join smaller strips with a diagonal seam (see Double-Fold Binding with Mitred Corners, page 141 step 3). If you have one, use a ½in (1.3cm) bias tape maker to turn under the raw edges (see tip below).

tip

When using a bias tape maker, the side with the slit down the middle should be uppermost and the end of the fabric strip pinned to the ironing board, wrong side up. Hold the side of the iron right next to the bias maker and pull it gradually along the strip.

27 Place the right side of the strip to the right side of the square, with the raw edges matching. Begin sewing the strip about 2in (5cm) before a corner, leaving a 6in (15.2cm) length of strip free at the beginning. Sew along the creased line of the strip, stopping at the corner on the diagonal seam of the puffing block. Pivot the block and sew off the corner (Fig 20). Fold the strip over so that the right side is uppermost and the other edge is turned under. Mark with a pin on the block where the edge of the tape lies (Fig 21). Fold the tape back down on the block as it was sewn. Fold up the tape in line with the diagonal seam (Fig 22) and then fold the tape back down just below the pin line (Fig 23). Pin along the next stitching line and check the mitre at the corner before continuing. Begin stitching again about ⅛in (3mm) from the top folded edge. Sew all the way around, stopping about 4in (10cm) from the beginning. Join the strip ends with a diagonal seam (see page 141 Double-Fold Binding with Mitred Corners) and complete the stitching.

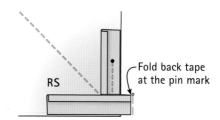

Fig 23

Fold back tape at the pin mark

RS

28 Fold the strip with right side uppermost and buttonhole appliqué stitch (or zigzag or blind hemstitch) around the outside edge of the strip (Fig 24). Cut the square to 15⅛in (38.4cm) – this includes a ½in (1.3cm) seam allowance. Your Puffing block is now finished: go on to make three more. See page 48 for the next quilt block.

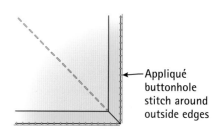

Appliqué buttonhole stitch around outside edges

Fig 24

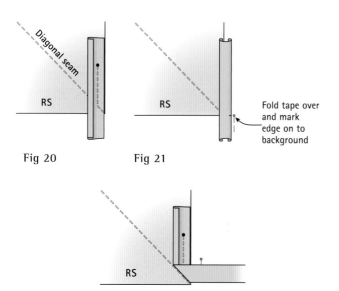

Fig 20 **Fig 21**

Diagonal seam

RS

RS

Fold tape over and mark edge on to background

RS

Fig 22

The Puffing block creates a wonderful, eye-catching effect on the Heirloom Quilt, especially with the three-dimensional tulip-shaped centres.

Heirloom
Pillow

This elegant project will give you the opportunity not only to create something beautiful but also to practise the techniques used in the Puffing blocks of the Heirloom Quilt. For the puffing strip, the light woven fabric required could be batiste or silk and preferably the same as the main fabric of your pillow. If you are using silk, cut it with the long edge parallel to the straight grain. If using cotton cut it with the long edge perpendicular to the straight grain. Test the two different grains first to see which gathers best. Shorter lengths can be joined with a narrow seam.

Finished size: 16in (40.6cm) long x 6in (15.2cm) diameter
Techniques: faggoting (page 126) • puffing (page 124)
wing needle sewing (page 112) • mirror imaging (page 127)
sewing over cord (page 109) • twin needle pin-tucks (page 129)
making and applying piping (page 141)

you will need

- Silk or cotton fabric, four strips 4⅝in x 22in (11.7cm x 56cm) and two strips for the ends, each 3½in x 20in (9cm x 51cm)
- Light woven fabric for the puffing strip 2in x 60in (5cm x 152.5cm)
- Ribbon 1½yd x ¼in or ⅛in (1.5m x 6mm or 3mm) to coordinate with main fabric, in width the same or less than the maximum width of your decorative stitches
- Ribbon 1½yd x ⅝in (1.5m x 15mm) or wider for behind faggoting
- Stranded cord 5yd (5m) approximately
- Two strips same as main fabric for piping 1½in x 22in (3.8cm x 56cm) (optional)
- Piping cord 1½yd (1.5m) x 4mm (optional)
- Rayon machine sewing thread to coordinate with fabric for decorative stitches, and bobbin thread to match fabric or top thread
- Bolster pillow form 16in x 6in (41cm x 15cm) – see Suppliers
- Two buttons 1½in (3.8cm) for covering, plus main fabric scraps to cover them
- Tear-away stabilizer
- Wing needle and 2.0 or 2.5mm twin needle
- Optional presser feet: gathering foot, cording foot, open-toe foot, wide groove piping foot, faggoting foot or Spanish hemstitching foot (see page 104)

Sewing the Faggoting and Puffing Strip

1 Use tear-away stabilizer when sewing all of the decorative stitches except for the faggoting and the twin needle pin-tucks. When marking the stitching guide lines, use a removable marker such as an air- or iron-erasable one. On the wrong sides of each of the four main strips, mark a line 1in (2.5cm) from one of the long edges. Fold the raw edge to the line, resulting in a ½in (1.3cm) hem, and iron flat.

2 Join the strips together in two pairs along the folded edges with faggoting (see page 126 Faggoting).

3 Machine tack (baste) a length of the wider ribbon behind the faggoting to keep the gap apart. Sew a scallop or decorative stitch of your choice either side of the faggoting with the inside edge of the open-toe foot running along the folded edge of the fabric. Make sure the stitch is close enough to the faggoting so that it catches the edges of the ribbon at the back.

4 Make the puffing strip from the long narrow strip (see page 124 Puffing). The finished length of the strip should be at least 22in (56cm) long. If it's longer the excess can be cut off after the next step.

5 Insert the puffing between the two panels with raw edges together and using a ½in (1.3cm) seam.

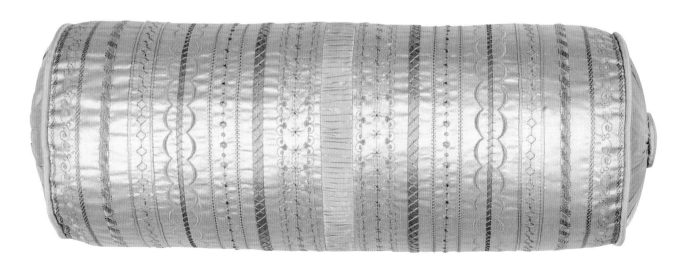

Adding the Decorative Stitches

6 As the decorative sewing either side of the puffing is the same for both sides, it is best to mark and sew each side at the same time rather than completing one side at a time. Draw a line halfway between the edge of the puffing and the edge of the scallop or decorative stitches next to the faggoting. Sew a row of decorative stitching over the narrow ribbon along the line.

7 Sew a row of wing needle stitches (see page 112 Wing Needle Sewing) halfway between the edge of the ribbon and the edge of the puffing. Sew a row of decorative stitches either side of the wing needle stitches. If the stitch is not symmetrical you will need to mirror image the stitch for one of the sides (see page 127 Mirror Imaging), or turn the fabric around and start from the other end.

8 Mark a line halfway between the edge of the scallop or decorative stitch next to the faggoting and the edge of the ribbon. Sew a decorative stitch along the line and then a wing needle stitch either side of the decorative stitch.

9 Draw a line halfway between the edge of the scallop or decorative stitches next to the faggoting and ½in (1.3cm) from the raw edge. Sew a decorative stitch over the stranded cord along the line (see page 109 Sewing over Cord).

10 Draw a line halfway between the edge of the scallop or decorative stitches next to the faggoting and the edge of the sewn cord. Sew a wing needle stitch along the line and then a row of twin needle pin-tucks (see page 129 Twin Needle Pin-tucks) either side of the wing needle stitches.

11 Draw a line halfway between the edge of the sewn cord and ½in (1.3cm) from the raw edge. Sew a row of decorative stitches along the line and then a row of wing needle or decorative stitches either side.

Finishing the Pillow

12 Trim the length of the rectangle to 20in (51cm). Along both short ends of the end strips, turn a double ¼in (6mm) hem to the wrong side. Machine sew the edge of the hem.

13 Now turn a double ¼in (6mm) hem to the wrong side along one long edge of the end strips and machine sew the edge of the hem.

14 Wrap the wrong side of the long fabric strip around the piping cord and using a piping foot or zipper foot, machine in place close to the cord. Trim the seam allowance of the piping to ½in (1.3cm). Machine tack (baste) the piping to the right side of one long edge of the rectangle, with raw edges matching (see page 141 Making and Applying Piping). The last two rows of tacking (basting) should be close to the piping but not right next to it.

tip

Having the last two rows of tacking close to the piping but not right next to it will prevent the stitching from showing when the piping has been inserted. The easiest way to do this is to move the needle position over slightly before you begin to sew.

15 On the edges that have the piping attached, place a mark ½in (1.3cm) in from both ends. Pin an end strip, right sides together and raw edges matching, to each edge of the pillow that has the piping, placing the finished end of the strips at the ½in (1.3cm) marks (Fig 1). Machine sew in place with a ½in (1.3cm) seam allowance, right next to the piping.

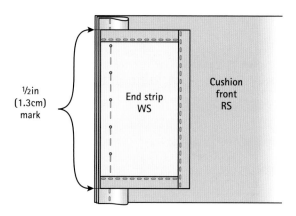

½in (1.3cm) mark

End strip WS

Cushion front RS

Fig 1

16 Fold the rectangle right sides together, matching the raw edges and forming a tube. Machine from the edge of the piping at both ends with a ½in (1.3cm) seam allowance. To prevent thread tails at the ends of the seam, begin about 1in (2.5cm) in from the starting end and sew towards the start. Leave the needle in the fabric, turn the fabric around 180° and sew to the end of the seam. Leave the needle in the fabric, turn it around 180° and sew to about 1in (2.5cm) from the end. Remove from the machine.

17 Press the seam open and turn through to the right side. Push the pillow form inside the tube. Thread a blunt needle with a length of stranded cord and thread this through the hem of the end strip. Pull the cord up as tightly as possible and knot securely. You will end up with a gap about 1in (2.5cm) diameter in the centre. Cover the button and sew it in the centre of the gap, catching the edges of the button down so that it covers the stitching on the hem. Sew the edges of the end strip closed if needed. Repeat for the other end and your pillow is finished.

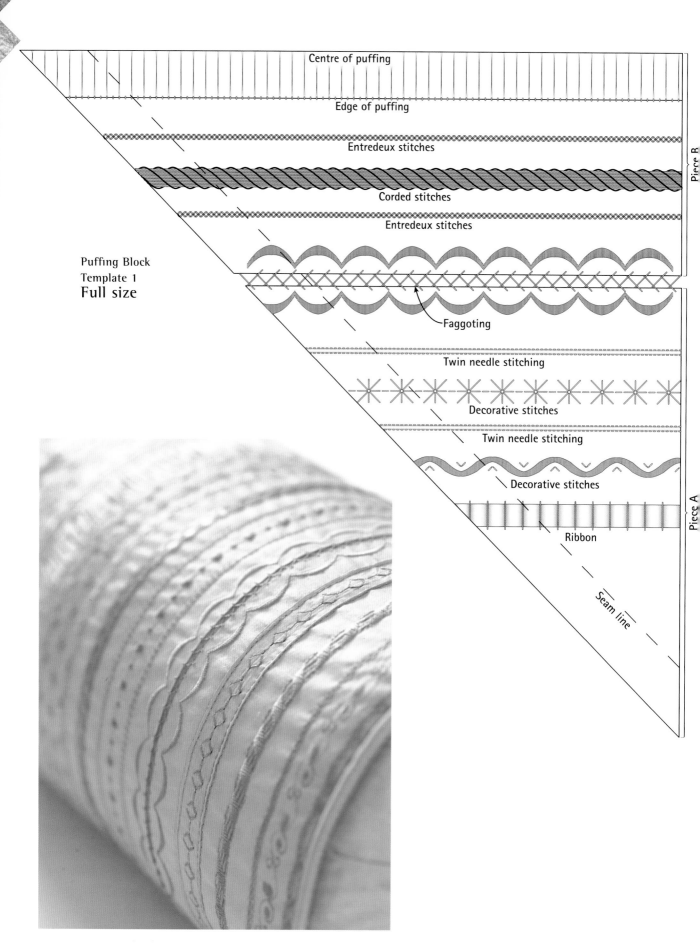

Centre of puffing

Edge of puffing

Entredeux stitches

Corded stitches

Entredeux stitches

Puffing Block
Template 1
Full size

Faggoting

Twin needle stitching

Decorative stitches

Twin needle stitching

Decorative stitches

Ribbon

Piece B

Piece A

Seam line

46

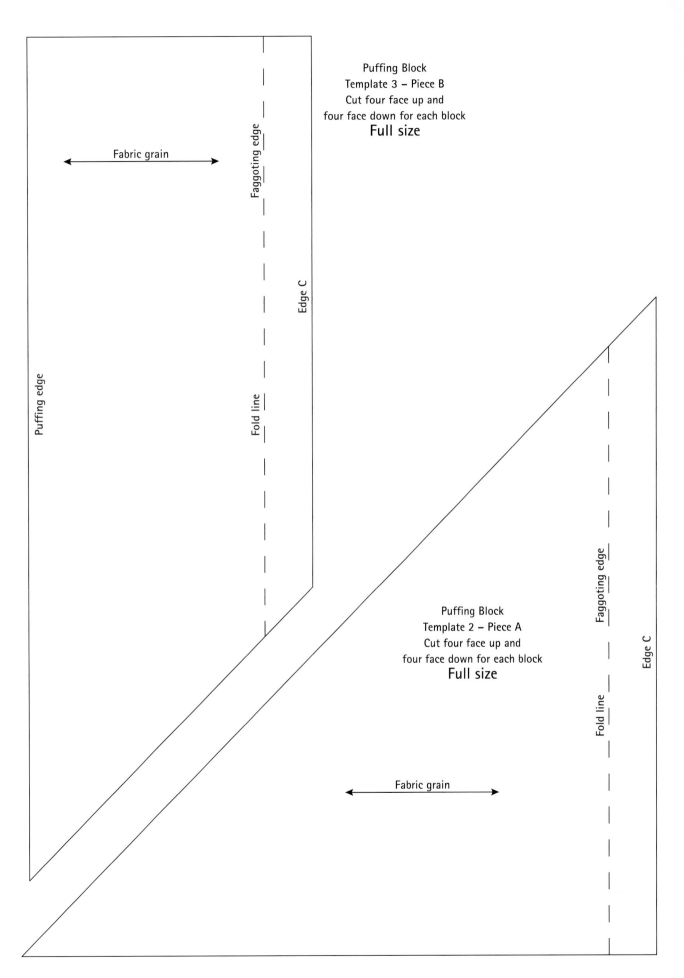

Fabric grain

Faggoting edge

Edge C

Puffing Block
Template 3 – Piece B
Cut four face up and
four face down for each block
Full size

Puffing edge

Fold line

Puffing Block
Template 2 – Piece A
Cut four face up and
four face down for each block
Full size

Faggoting edge

Edge C

Fold line

Fabric grain

Cutwork Block

you will need
(to make two blocks multiply the amounts given by two)

Once you have mastered the technique for sewing a cutwork design with Richelieu bars there will be no stopping you! It can be adapted and used on clothing as well as soft furnishings. Experiment with different fabrics peeping through the cutwork: satin or lamé would be stunning on an evening bag – ooh, I feel a course coming on! There are two Cutwork blocks in the Heirloom Quilt and the directions are for making one of them. To make two, double the requirements in the You Will Need list. Templates are given full size on page 57. If you want to practise the techniques first, start with the useful covered box on page 52.

- Calico or chosen background fabric 18in (46cm) square
- Wadding (batting) 18in (46cm) square
- Silk in dark shade ¼yd (0.25m) x 45in (115cm)
- Silk in medium shade ⅛yd (0.15m) x 45in (115cm)
- Fusible interfacing ⅛yd (0.15m) x 36in (90cm)
- Four lace motifs no larger than 2in x 2½in (5cm x 6cm) in a shell, circle, kite or oval shape (see page 121 for examples)
- Fusible web such as Bondaweb (Wonder Under) 18in x 12in (46cm x 30cm)
- Thin water-soluble stabilizer (such as Solvy) two 8in (20.3cm) squares
- Tear-away stabilizer
- Embroidery hoop 6in (15cm) diameter
- Machine needle size 60 or 70
- Open-toe foot
- Bead for the centre (5mm–6mm diameter)
- Threads: 40 weight rayon machine embroidery to match dark silk; 40 weight rayon machine embroidery to match medium silk; machine thread for bobbin and machine thread to match lace
- Point turner (optional)

Finished size of block: 15⅛in x 15⅛in (38.4cm x 38.4cm), includes ½in (1.3cm) seam allowance for quilt assembly
Techniques: satin stitch appliqué (page 116) • sewing lace motifs (page 121) • sewing two curved sides that meet at a point (page 111) • cutwork (page 122) • finished-edge appliqué (page 114) • candlewicking by machine (page 113)

Preparing the Appliqués

1 Fold the background square in half diagonally and iron to make a crease. Open out and fold the other way diagonally and make another crease.

2 Trace around the large shell shape Template 1 on page 57 four times on the paper side of the fusible web and roughly cut out each shell shape (Fig 1). Place the shapes, sticky side down on the wrong side of the dark shade of silk (Fig 2). Make sure they will all fit before you fuse them in place. Cut out each shell shape on the drawn line.

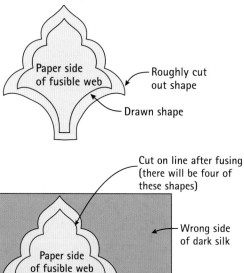

Fig 2

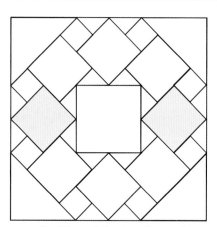

Position of the two Cutwork blocks in the Heirloom Quilt

3 Peel off the paper backing from the fusible web and place the shells centrally over the creases on the background fabric, with the tip at the top of each shell 8½in (21.6cm) from the centre. Check to make sure that opposite tips are 17in (43.2cm) apart and that the base of each shell is centred over the crease. Press carefully to fuse in place (Fig 3).

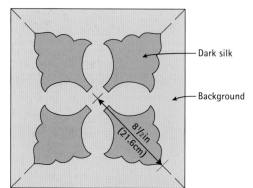

Fig 3

48

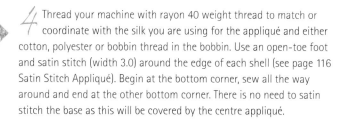

4 Thread your machine with rayon 40 weight thread to match or coordinate with the silk you are using for the appliqué and either cotton, polyester or bobbin thread in the bobbin. Use an open-toe foot and satin stitch (width 3.0) around the edge of each shell (see page 116 Satin Stitch Appliqué). Begin at the bottom corner, sew all the way around and end at the other bottom corner. There is no need to satin stitch the base as this will be covered by the centre appliqué.

5 On the smooth (non-sticky) side of the fusible interfacing, draw four small shells using Template 2 on page 57, leaving about 1in (2.5cm) between the shapes. Pin this, sticky-side down to the right side of the medium shade silk. Sew around each shape on the drawn line with a small straight stitch. There is no need to sew along the bottom edge of the shells. Cut out each shell approximately ⅛in (3mm) from the stitching line. Snip the seam allowances at the inside points and trim the seam allowances at the outer points. Cut a slit in the middle of the interfacing and turn the shapes through to the right side. Use a point turner to define the points and the curves by running it along the seam inside. Tack (baste) the edges in place. Do *not* iron.

6 Pin the small shells on top of the large shells so the tips are 1¼in (3.2cm) away from the tips of the large shells. Using a pressing sheet, lightly press in place and remove the tacking (basting) stitches. Because the sticky side of the interfacing is on the back of the small shell shape, it will stick to the larger shell. Turn the square over and press the shapes from the wrong side of the background. Appliqué in place using a thread to match the small shells (see page 114 Finished-Edge Appliqué).

Applying the Lace Motifs and Echo Quilting

7 Pin a lace motif to each small shell, making sure the top edges are all the same distance from the tips of the large shells. Sew in place (see page 121 Sewing Lace Motifs). If you can't find lace motifs and own an embroidery unit for your machine, you can purchase lace designs that are sewn on either organza or water-soluble stabilizer. Another option is to sew different decorative stitches in an oval shape as I have on the box project on page 52.

8 Pin and tack (baste) the wadding (batting) to the wrong side of the background. Use candlewicking (see page 113 Candlewicking by Machine) or a small decorative stitch to sew around the outside of each large shell. Guide the edge of the foot along the edge of the shell to keep the same distance away (see page 133 Echo Quilting). Sew the same stitch in the ovals between the shells, keeping the same distance away from the edge of the shells (Fig 4).

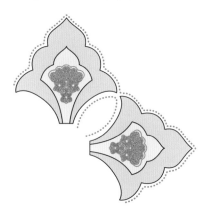

Fig 4

The cutwork centre to this block is a very attractive feature of the quilt, especially with the detailing of the Richelieu bars.

The shell shapes are outlined in candlewicking stitches, bringing even more texture to the Cutwork block.

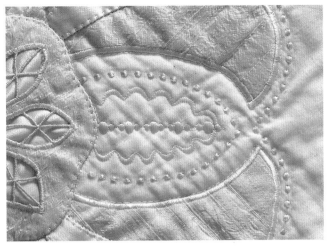

Making the Cutwork Centre

10 For the cutwork design, on an 8in (20.3cm) square of tear-away stabilizer, trace the red lines from the cutwork Template 3 on page 57. Place this, drawn side up, on top of an 8in (20.3cm) square of thin water-soluble stabilizer and then place an 8in (20.3cm) square of dark shade silk, wrong side up, underneath. Secure the three layers in a 6in (15cm) embroidery hoop by putting the smaller ring of the hoop on top of the tear-away stabilizer and clipping the outer ring underneath the silk. If your silk is very fine, iron a piece of fusible interfacing to the wrong side before placing it in the hoop. Follow the technique instructions for cutwork on page 122, sewing the Richelieu bars marked in black on the template. Remove the hoop and leave the tear-away stabilizer in place but remove as much of the water-soluble stabilizer as possible (see tip below). If you find this cutwork technique a little difficult, try the easier centre used on the box on page 54.

9 In the spaces between the shells mark an oval about ½in (1.3cm) inside the previous stitching (Fig 5). Begin at the top and sew a scallop or decorative stitch down either side of each marked oval (Fig 6). (See page 111 Sewing Two Curved Sides That Meet at a Point.) Mark a line going vertically down the centre of each oval and sew a decorative stitch along the line beginning just above the point at the top of the oval (Fig 7). This will cover up a point that may not be perfect!

tip

Remove water-soluble stabilizer by tearing it away. If any specks remain around the stitching, simply run a wet cotton bud (or Q-tip) around the edges to dissolve the stabilizer.

Fig 5

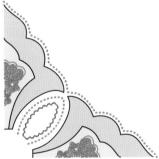

Fig 6

Fig 7

11 Place a 6in (15.2cm) square of silk (the same shade as used for the cutwork) under the cutwork, right sides together. With the wrong side of the cutwork on top, machine a straight stitch around the outside of the shape on the marked line on the tear-away stabilizer. Remove the tear-away stabilizer.

12 Place a contrasting 6in (15.2cm) square of silk underneath the cutwork, with the right side of the silk facing the wrong side of the cutwork. You should have a contrasting silk square on the bottom, right side up, the cutwork design on top of that, right side up and a piece of silk on the top, wrong side up. The two silk pieces on top are the same shade and are sewn together around the outline of the shape. Using a straight stitch, length 2.0, machine just inside the previous stitching through all the layers.

13 Trim close to the outside edge, clipping in at the corners. Make a slit in the centre of the silk that is the same shade as the cutwork, *not* the contrasting one. Turn the shape through to the right side. Press and appliqué the cutwork on the centre of the square (see page 114 Finished-Edge Appliqué).

14 Trim the square to 15⅛in (38.4cm) – this includes a ½in (1.3cm) seam allowance. Your Cutwork block is now finished: go on to make one more. See page 58 for the next quilt block.

Elegant Cutwork Box

For the top of this box I have chosen a slightly different centre, similar to reverse appliqué, which is a little easier than the technique used in the Cutwork block. However, you could make the top exactly the same as the Cutwork block if you wish. The box is perfect for storing the finished squares of your Heirloom Quilt and, would you believe, is sewn together on the machine!

Finished size of box: 20in x 20in x 4in (50.8cm x 50.8cm x 10.2cm)
Techniques: satin stitch appliqué (page 116) • sewing two curved sides that meet at a point (page 111) • cutwork (page 122) finished-edge appliqué (page 114) • candlewicking by machine (page 113)

Cutting out the Card and Fabric

1 Draw the following shapes on the mounting board sheets using a ruler and pencil. Write the dimensions and name in the centre of each one. Fig 1 gives guidance on fitting the shapes on the sheets.

Outside base	20in x 20in (50.8cm x 50.8cm) draw one.
Outside base sides	20in x 4in (50.8cm x 10.2cm) draw two.
Outside base sides	20¼in x 4in (51.4cm x 10.2cm) draw two.
Outside lid	20½in x 20½in (52cm x 52cm) draw one.
Outside lid sides	20½in x 1½in (52cm x 3.8cm) draw two.
Outside lid sides	20¾in x 1½in (52.7cm x 3.8cm) draw two.
Inside base	19¾in x 19¾in (50.2cm x 50.2cm) draw one.
Inside base sides	19¾in x 3¾in (50.2cm x 9.5cm) draw two.
Inside base sides	20in x 3¾in (50.8cm x 9.5cm) draw two.
Inside lid	20¼in x 20¼in (51.4cm x 51.4cm) draw one.
Inside lid sides	20¼in x 1¼in (51.4cm x 3.2cm) draw two.
Inside lid sides	20½in x 1¼in (52cm x 3.2cm) draw two.

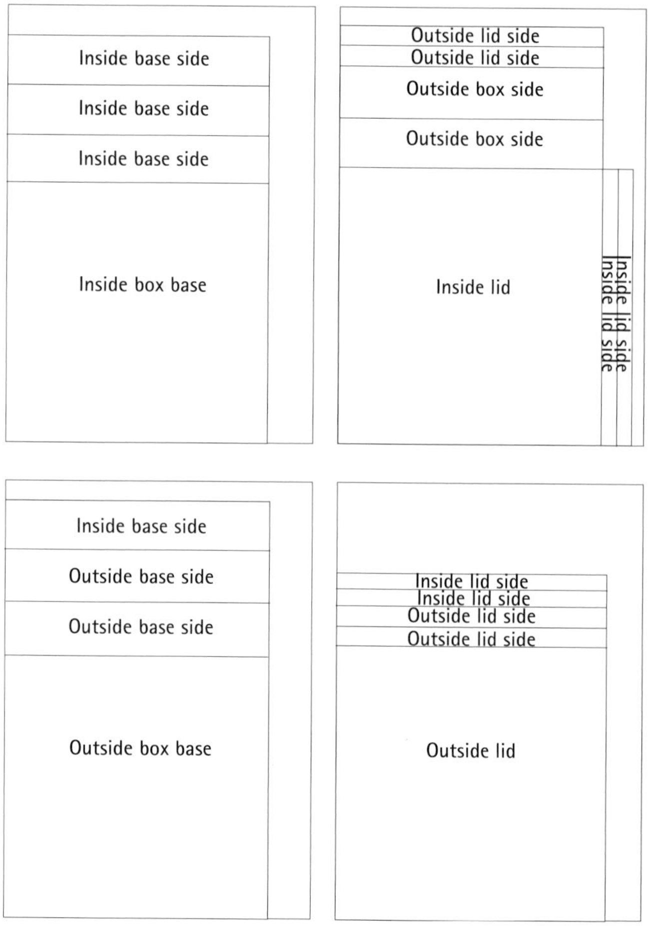

you will need

- Four A1 sheets of mounting board, each 33in x 24¼in (83.8cm x 61.5cm)
- Fabric for outside of box 1⅓yd x 45in wide (1.2m x 115cm)
- Fabric for inside of box 1⅓yd x 45in wide (1.2m x 115cm)
- Roll of double-sided tape ½in (1.3cm) wide
- Rotary cutter, long ruler, large cutting mat and masking tape
- Silk in dark shade ¼yd (0.25m)
- Silk in medium shade ⅛yd (0.15m)
- Fusible interfacing ⅛yd (0.15m)
- Four lace motifs no larger than 2in x 2½in (5cm x 6.3cm) in shell, circle, kite or oval shape (optional) – see page 121 for examples
- Fusible web such as Bondaweb (Wonder Under) 18in x 12in (44cm x 30cm)
- Thin water-soluble stabilizer (such as Solvy) two 8in (20.3cm) squares
- Tear-away stabilizer
- Embroidery hoop 6in (15cm) diameter
- Machine needle size 60 or 70
- Open-toe foot
- Candlewicking foot (optional)
- Threads: 40 weight rayon machine embroidery to match dark silk; 40 weight rayon machine embroidery to match medium silk; machine thread for bobbin and machine thread to match lace (if using)
- Wadding (batting) 22in (56cm) square

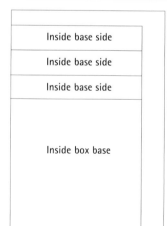

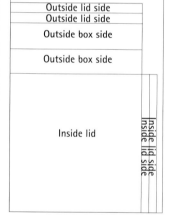

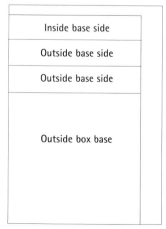

Fig 1

2 Using a long ruler, rotary cutter and cutting mat, cut out all the shapes. Place all the shapes on the corresponding fabric leaving about 2in (5cm) between them. Cut the fabric between the shapes making sure you leave enough fabric around the edges for turnings, about 1in (2.5cm) on the large squares and ¾in (2cm) on the others.

Decorating the Box Top

3 Using the fabric cut for the outside lid and the dark and medium shade of silk, follow the directions for the Cutwork block for the design on the top (steps 1–13 beginning on page 48) if you wish the box to look the same as the Cutwork block. If you are unable to find lace motifs suitable then you could sew a row of decorative stitches in an oval shape as I have.

4 For an alternative cutwork centre, follow step 10 on page 57 of the Cutwork block, replacing the water-soluble stabilizer with a square of contrasting fabric and omitting the Richelieu bars. You only need to cut away the top layer of silk, leaving the contrasting fabric and the tear-away stabilizer intact. Follow steps 11–13 on page 51 (but omitting the contrasting fabric, which has already been applied). to complete the shape. The picture below shows the near finished look – all that is required is to add a decorative stitch at the outer points of each petal.

5 Pin and then tack (baste) the wadding (batting) centrally to the wrong side of the decorated fabric for the box top.

6 To centre the design on the lid, draw diagonal lines from corner to corner on the wrong side, as shown below and place the lid shape on top so the corners are on the lines. Draw around the lid, remove it and cut the wadding around the square.

This shows the wrong side of the whole design, with the diagonal guidelines for placing the card centrally over the design.

Applying the Fabric to the Card

7 Place each shape on the wrong side of the corresponding piece of fabric. Stick a small length of double-sided tape at each corner and fold the fabric over. Stick tape along each side and fold the fabric over the sides (Fig 2).

This shows the easier version of the cutwork centre on the box, without the Richelieu bars. Decorative stitches will be added to the outer points of each petal.

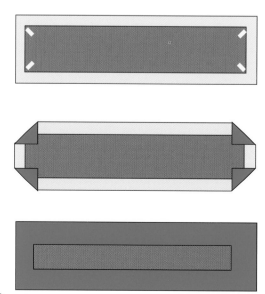

Fig 2

Sewing the Pieces Together

8 Gather the five pieces that make up the inside base. Beginning with the two shorter sides, place one of them next to a side of the base, right sides uppermost, making sure the top and bottom edges are level. Stick strips of masking tape across to hold the two pieces in place (see Fig 2). Thread your machine with a matching thread in the top and bobbin and select a bridging stitch (Fig 3), width 3.0 or a zigzag stitch (length 3.0, width 3.0). Use a ditch-stitching foot or edge-joining foot if you have one, or an open-toe foot. Carefully sew the two pieces together guiding the centre of the foot in between them and securing the threads at the beginning and end. You may have to stand up when you begin to sew as the box pieces are rather large.

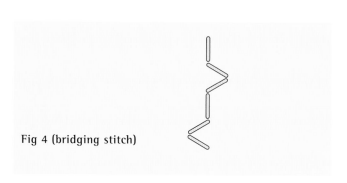

Fig 4 (bridging stitch)

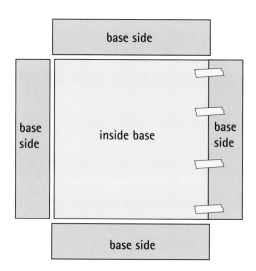

Fig 2

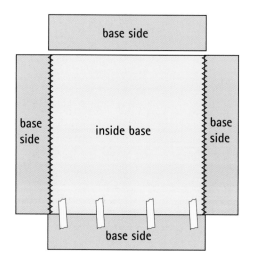

Fig 3

9 Sew the other shorter side to the opposite side of the base in the same way. The two remaining sides are sewn in the same way but are a little longer than the base. These should be placed so that they extend the same amount at each end.

10 Now sew the inside lid of the box, the outside lid and the outside base together by machine in the same way.

11 Hand sew each corner closed, bringing wrong sides together for the outside base and lid and right sides together for the inside base and lid.

12 Stick a strip of double-sided adhesive tape about ⅛in (3mm) below each top edge of the inside base and inside lid on the wrong side. Do not remove the backing strip yet. Place the inside base inside the outside base. Carefully remove the backing strips from the double-sided tape and press the sides together to stick. Repeat for the lid. Your box is now finished.

tip

If you want to make a box in a different size it is easy to calculate the dimesions of each template. My box is 20in x 20in x 4in (50.8cm x 50.8cm x 10.2cm) and each template is based on that size and is either a little larger, smaller or the same. All you need to do is add or take away that same measurement from your basic size. For example, if you are making a box 14in x 14in x 6in (35.5cm x 35.5cm x 15.2cm) then the outiside lid will measure 14½in x 14½in (36.8cm x 36.8cm) and the inside base sides will measure 13¾in x 5¾in (34.9cm x 14.6cm).

Cutwork Block
Template 1
Full size

Cutwork Block
Template 2
Full size

Cutwork Block
Template 3
Full size

Trapunto Corner Block

Trapunto is also called stuffed quilting and is one of my favourite techniques. It's so bold and 'squidgy', and very rewarding to do. There are four trapunto blocks in the Heirloom Quilt – perfect for framing the quilt at the corners. The directions are for making one corner block. To make four, quadruple the requirements in the You Will Need list. The list is for one corner as the background for each one is made from a triangle that is half a 25in (63.5cm) square cut in half diagonally. Template 4 on page 67 has been reduced – follow the instructions there to enlarge it to full size.

Finished size of block: 21⅝in (55cm) square cut in half diagonally, includes ½in (1.3cm) seam allowance for quilt assembly
Techniques: couching (page 111) • finished-edge appliqué (page 114) • machine trapunto (page 140) • Italian quilting (page 132) machine quilting (page 131) • triple stitch (page 109)

Preparing the Appliqués

1 From the silk for the appliqué shapes, cut out half a 7in (17.8cm) circle and the same from the fusible interfacing. Use Template 1 on page 66 (it is given full size) and draw the cording pattern and outside shape on the right side of the silk half circle with an air-erasable marker, centring it and leaving a border around the outside. Place tear-away stabilizer underneath.

2 Use a rayon thread in the top of the machine to match the cord and a narrow braid/cord foot and guide or open-toe foot. Select a zigzag stitch, adjusted to a length and width to cover the cord and couch the cord on the drawn line (see page 111 Couching). Leave the tails free below the base line (Fig 1).

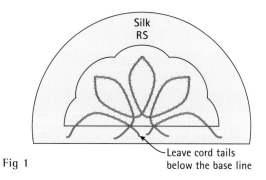

Silk RS

Fig 1   Leave cord tails below the base line

3 On the wrong side of the half circle, trace the outside line of the design. Place the smooth side of the fusible interfacing under the right side of the silk. Using a straight stitch, length 2.0, and polyester thread to match the silk, sew around the outside of the design beginning along the base line, not at a corner.

4 Trim the seam allowance to within ⅛in (3mm) of the stitching. Clip the corners and inside points. Make a 1in (2.5cm) slit in the centre of the interfacing and turn the shape through to the right side.

you will need

(to make four blocks multiply the amounts given by four)

- Dark shade of silk for the appliqué shapes 7in x 12in (18cm x 30.5cm)
- Medium shade of silk or calico, half 25in (64cm) square (cut diagonally) for the background
- Quilt wadding, half 25in (64cm) square (cut diagonally)
- Fusible interfacing 7in x 12in (18cm x 30.5cm) and half 25in (64cm) square (cut diagonally) – enough for two blocks
- Polyester wadding (batting) 4oz (135g) or similar lofty wadding, half 16in (40.5cm) square (cut diagonally)– enough for two blocks
- Rayon cord or similar 9yd (8m) approximately
- Quilting wool 5yd (5m) (or 25g skein for four blocks)
- Small amount of toy stuffing
- Long needle with a large eye
- Threads: rayon thread to match the cord and the appliqué shapes; machine sewing thread to match both fabrics; thread for the background quilting
- Walking foot, narrow braid/cord foot and guide or open-toe foot (optional)
- Tear-away stabilizer
- Quilter's ruler 24in (60cm)
- Eight tiny beads (optional)
- Air-erasable fabric marker or similar

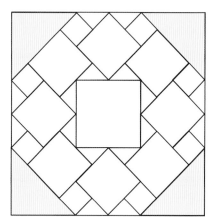

Position of the four Trapunto Corner blocks in the Heirloom Quilt

Use a blunt point to go around the edge of the shape on the inside to define the curves. Press carefully to fuse the interfacing to the wrong side of the silk, making sure the interfacing doesn't show on the right side around the edge.

5 On the wrong side of the dark silk, draw around the shell shape given in Template 2 on page 66 (it is given full size). On the wrong side, draw the half shell shape using Template 3 (given full size). Flip the half shell template over and draw around it again at least ½in (1.3cm) away from the other half shape. Roughly cut out all three shapes, leaving at least ¼in (6mm) around the outside edges.

6 Place a piece of fusible interfacing under each shape, with the smooth side of the interfacing under the right side of the shapes. Make sure you have a left and right half shell.

7 Sew around the lines on the silk, beginning at the bottom corner and finishing at the opposite bottom corner. Do not sew along the base line of the shapes.

8 Trim the seam allowance to within ⅛in (3mm) of the stitching. Clip the corners and inside points. Make a 1in (2.5cm) slit in the centre of the interfacing and turn the shapes through to the right side. If you have a tube turner use it to turn the half shells. Use a blunt point to go around the edge of the shapes on the inside to define the curves. Press carefully to fuse, making sure the interfacing doesn't show on the right side around the edge.

Sewing the Trapunto

9 Fold the background triangle in half and press to give a centre line. Open out the triangle and use an erasable marker to trace the design from Template 4 on page 67 on to the left side on the front of the fabric (enlarging the template first by 166.6% to full size). The base line should be 2in (5cm) from the bottom cut edge of the fabric, and the centre line on the pattern on the centre crease. Do not trace the inner appliqué shell shapes. To trace the right-hand side, either mirror image the design on a photocopier or turn the template over and trace the lines on to the back using a light box or tape it to a window to see the lines.

tip

If using an air-erasable marking pen make sure you have time to complete the block before it disappears! If not, then a grey quilter's pencil works well.

10 Pin the polyester wadding (batting) under the triangle, making sure that it is under the large shell shape and the half shell shapes. Using a straight stitch, length 3.5, a walking foot and thread to match the background, sew around the outside of the large shell shape, the red line marked on the template, including the line at the base of the shell (see page 140 Machine Trapunto, method 2).

11 Turn the background to the wrong side and cut the wadding close to the outside of the stitching. Sew around the large half shell shapes with the polyester wadding underneath and trim them as before.

12 Iron the half square of fusible interfacing to the quilt wadding and pin this to the wrong side of the background, with the interfacing facing the outside.

Applying the Appliqués

13 Pin the small shell in the centre of the large shell on the background so the point at the top is 1½in (3.8cm) from the point of the large shell (Fig 2). Pin the half shells in place – they should sit a fraction above the base line. The ends of the appliqué shapes will extend under where the half circle will be attached.

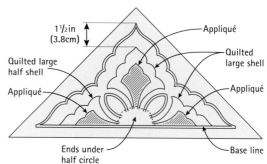

Fig 2

14 Thread your machine with a colour that matches the appliqué fabric and sew the shapes to the background using a buttonhole appliqué stitch or similar (see page 114 Finished-Edge Appliqué). Make sure you pin the half shells very well beforehand and sew these along the base line first.

15 Thread your machine with a colour that matches the cord and select a zigzag stitch adjusted to a length and width that will cover the cord. You may also need to lower the foot pressure a little if the foot drags when sewing the cord. Attach either a walking foot or braiding foot. Beginning at the base of one of the inner ovals that is between the centre shell and half shell shapes, leave a 1in (2.5cm) tail of cord and couch the cord around the line (see page 111 Couching). Leave a 1in (2.5cm) thread tail at the end and cut the cord. Repeat for the other inner oval and both outer ovals. Couch the cord around the outside of the large shell, leaving thread tails as before at the base. For the half shells, begin at the corner of the shape on the base line, couch around the shape and finish at the other end of the shape at the base line without couching along the base line itself. Use a needle with a large eye to pull the cord ends at the points of the half shells only through to the back. The other cord ends will be covered by the half circle appliqué.

16 Make a 1in (2.5cm) slit in the background through all layers under where the half circle will go. Pin the half circle to the background, positioning it a fraction above the base line to give room for couching the cord and appliqué around the edge the same as you did for the shell shapes.

17 Couch cord around both sides of the channel on the outside of the design, sewing the inner one first. Pull the ends of the cord through to the back as before.

The Trapunto Corner blocks on the Heirloom Quilt bring a gorgeous three-dimensional quality to the quilt and contrast beautifully with the densely quilted borders.

Quilting the Background

18 For the background quilting, you will need to draw vertical and horizontal lines on the front of the triangle using an air-erasable marker or similar (Fig 3). Do not draw any lines on the shell shapes, the centre half circle or the corded channels of the oval and outside. Draw the first line 1in (2.5cm) below the lower corded line (the baseline marked on the template) – this is the seam line.

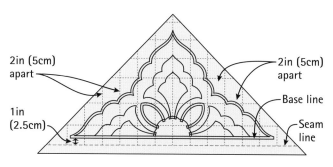

2in (5cm) apart

2in (5cm) apart

Base line

1in (2.5cm)

Seam line

Fig 3

19 Draw another line down the centre of the triangle from the point at the top to the seam line at the base. Using the centre line as guide, draw lines 2in (5cm) apart either side, each one ending at the seam line. Using the seam line as a guide, draw lines above it, 2in (5cm) apart, to the top of the triangle.

20 Using a walking foot, machine quilting thread in the top and a straight stitch length 3.0, sew along all the lines except the seam line. Secure the stitches at the beginning and end of each line.

21 Draw a set of lines between the 2in (5cm) lines and quilt these as before. Your stitched lines will be 1in (2.5cm) apart. Draw another set of lines between these and quilt. Your stitched lines will now be ½in (1.3cm) apart, with one horizontal line sewn below the base line.

22 On the inside of the ovals, mark and quilt lines between the sewn lines, making the final stitching ¼in (6mm) apart in these areas.

Stuffing the Channels and Half Circle

23 Cut a 4yd (3.6m) length of quilting wool and thread this through a long blunt needle with a large eye. Bring the two ends of the wool level as you will be threading two strands through the channel at the same time. Stuff the outside channel between the wadding and the background fabric with the two lengths (see page 132 Italian Quilting). Do the same for the oval channels using a 12in (30.5cm) length of wool for each one.

24 Stuff the half circle lightly with toy stuffing through the background slit. Hand sew the slit closed.

25 Mark a line down the centre of the appliquéd shell beginning 2in (5cm) from the point and ending at the edge where it meets the half circle. Use a triple stitch (see page 109) (or straight stitch) with rayon thread in the top and sew down the line. Sew a triple stitch down the centre of the loops on the half circle, stopping ½in (1.3cm) from the top of each loop.

Completing the Block

26 Sew three beads on the base line at the centre of the half circle, three beads at the top of the triple stitching on the appliquéd shell and one bead on each appliquéd half shell 2in (5cm) from the point on the base line.

27 Trim the finished corner to half a 21⅝in (55cm) square, making sure the lower cut edge of the triangle is ½in (1.3cm) below the seam line at the bottom. Your Trapunto corner block is now finished: go on to make three more. See page 68 for the next block.

Trapunto Cushion

An elegant pillow can be created by joining two of the trapunto corners as used in the Heirloom Quilt in a square design. The edges are then piped and bound. I have used two gold shades of silk but feel free to select any two fabrics that grab you! Tone-on-tone cotton, chintz, satin, even one floral and the other plain would all work well.

Finished size of cushion: 18in x 18in (45.7cm x 45.7cm)
Techniques: couching (page 111) • finished-edge appliqué (page 114) • machine trapunto (page 140) • Italian quilting (page 132) • machine quilting (page 131) • making and applying piping (page 141) • triple stitching (page 109)

you will need

- Fabric A ¼yd x 45in wide (0.25m x 115cm wide) approx, for the appliqué shapes and piping
- Fabric B 1yd x 45in wide (1m x 115cm wide) for background, binding and backs
- Polyester wadding (batting) or similar lofty wadding 16in (40.5cm) square of 4oz (135g)
- Fusible interfacing 7in x 24in (18cm x 61cm) plus one 21in (53.3cm) square
- Quilt wadding (batting) 21in (53.3cm) square
- Thin cord or six-stranded embroidery thread 15yd (15m) approximately for couching
- Calico or similar 21in (53.3cm) square, to back the front
- Quilting wool 9yd (9m) approximately
- Small amount of toy stuffing
- Piping cord 4mm x 2¼yd (2.25m)
- Long needle with a large eye
- Threads: rayon machine embroidery thread to match the cord and fabric A and machine sewing thread to match both fabrics and for background quilting
- Air-erasable fabric marker
- Tear-away stabilizer
- Cushion pad 18in (46cm) square
- Walking foot, narrow braid/cord foot and guide or open-toe foot
- Quilter's ruler 24in (60cm)
- Tiny beads (twenty-seven)

Preparing the Appliqués

1 Using fabric A and the 7in x 24in (18cm x 61cm) piece of fusible interfacing, follow the directions for the Trapunto Corner block and make four large shell appliqué shapes (see steps 5–8 beginning on page 58). For the centre, make a complete circle by using Template 1 on page 66 (it is given full size). Couch the cord for the loops, threading the ends through to the back before completing the shape (see steps 1–4 on page 58).

Sewing the Trapunto

2 Cut a 21in (53.3cm) square from fabric B. Fold it in quarters and crease to mark the centre. Open out and fold it in half diagonally in both directions and crease again. This gives guidelines for marking the pattern. Draw the pattern on the front of the square, using Template 4 (enlarge the template by 166.6%). Place the corner blue lines shown on the template at the centre each time and the centre lines on the template along the diagonal creases. Note: you will have to mirror image the template for two of the four drawings. The centre of the oval shapes should be in line with the side creases on the background fabric.

3 Continue following the directions for the trapunto corner blocks to apply the polyester wadding (batting) beneath the four large shells (steps 10–11 on page 60). Cut the wadding away as directed.

4 Iron the square of fusible interfacing to the quilt wadding square and pin this to the wrong side of the background, with the interfacing facing the outside.

Applying the Appliqués and Quilting

5 Pin the small shells in the centre of the large shells on the background, so the point at the top is 1½in (3.8cm) from the point of the large shell, and appliqué in place. (Refer to page 114 Finished-Edge Appliqué).

6 Couch the cord around the large shells, the ovals and the outside channels (see page 111 Couching).

7 Quilt the background as described in the Trapunto corner block, steps 18–22 opposite.

Stuffing the Channels and Circle

8 Thread two strands of quilting wool through the outside channel and the four oval channels between the wadding and the background fabric using a long blunt needle with a large eye. See Italian Quilting page 132.

9 At this point you may need to manipulate the square slightly with the iron. If the square has become a little distorted, place it right side up on a flat surface that can be ironed on and pat it flat. Using a steam iron *lightly* press it flat around the outside of the stuffed shapes. Be careful not to hold the iron too close to the trapunto otherwise all your stuffing work will be lost.

10 Pin the 21in (53cm) square of calico or similar to the back of the cushion top and machine baste around the outside edge to keep the layers together. This layer will also help to keep the shape flat.

11 Cut a 1in (2.5cm) slit in the background through all layers in the middle of where the centre circle appliqué will be sewn.

Pin the circle to the cushion top, positioning it centrally and appliqué around the edge the same as for the shell shapes.

12 Stuff the circle lightly with toy stuffing through the slit in the background. Hand sew the slit closed.

13 Mark a line down the centre of each appliquéd shell beginning 2in (5cm) from the point and ending at the edge where they meet the circle. Use a triple stitch (see page 109) (or a straight stitch) with rayon thread in the top and sew down the line. Sew a triple stitch (or straight stitch) down the centre of the loops on the circle, stopping ½in (1.3cm) from the top of each loop.

Completing the Pillow Front

14 Sew three beads at the top of the triple stitching on the appliquéd shells, and one bead on each loop on the centre circle at the top of the triple stitching. Sew seven beads in the centre of the circle. Trim the finished top to 19in (48.3cm) square.

Making Up the Cushion

15 Cut two rectangles from fabric B, each 19in x 13in (48.3cm x 33cm). Make the pieces for the cushion back by turning under a ½in (1.3cm) double hem to the wrong side on one long edge of each back piece. Machine the two hems near the edge (see Fig 2 on page 27). Place the back pieces on your work surface, wrong sides up and overlap them until they are the same width as the cushion front. Pin the cushion front on top, right side up. Using a walking foot, sew around the edge with a long straight stitch about ¼in (6mm) from the raw edges (see Fig 3 on page 27).

16 Cut four strips from fabric A, each measuring 21in x 1½in (53.3cm x 3.8cm) for the piping. For the binding, cut four strips from fabric B, each measuring 21in x 2½in (53.3cm x 6.3cm).

17 Cover the piping cord and trim it to ⅜in (1cm) from the stitching line. Attach one strip to each side of the front of the cushion top – see page 141 Making and Applying Piping. Cut the ends of the piping level with the sides.

18 Fold each binding strip in half, wrong sides together and iron. Pin one strip to one edge of the cushion top over the piping, making raw edges level and leaving about 1in (2.5cm) extending at each end. Machine so that the stitches are right next to the edge of the piping that is under the binding. Pin and sew another strip to the opposite edge of the cushion in the same way.

This gorgeous cushion would be the ideal project to experiment with different fabrics and colours. Try shot dupion, velvet or satin. Two shades of marbled or tone-on-tone quilting cotton would also look very effective.

19 Cut the two ends of the binding level with the sides. Fold over the binding to the back of the cushion. Hand sew the folded edge of the binding just over the stitching line. Repeat step 18 for the remaining two sides.

20 Turn the two ends of the binding to the back and then fold over the binding strip to the back of the cushion. Hand sew the folded edge of the binding just over the stitching line. Insert the cushion pad to finish.

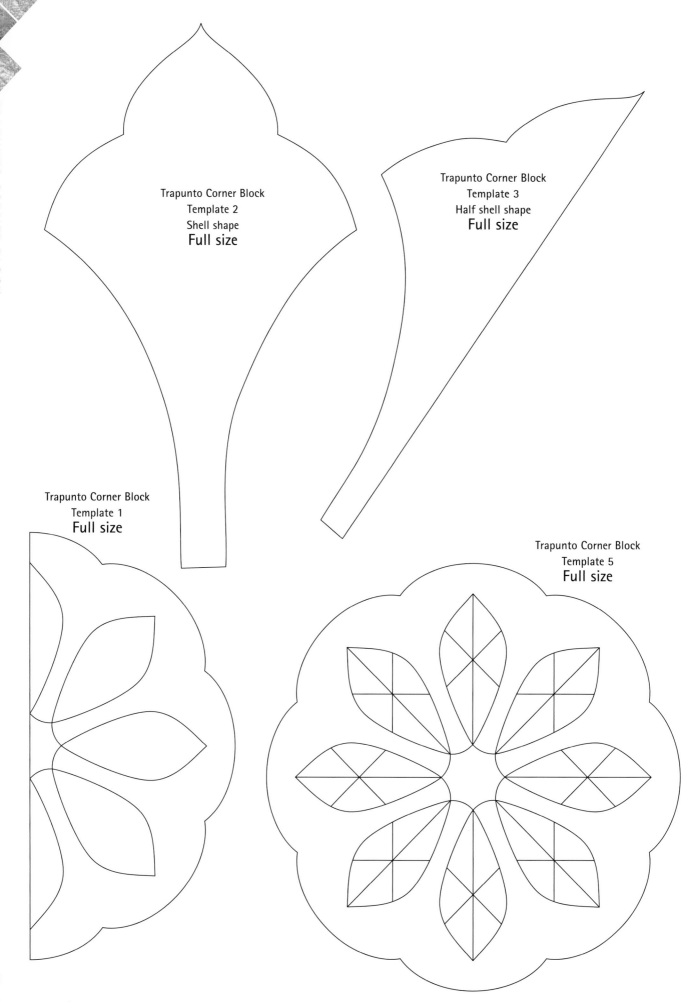

Trapunto Corner Block
Template 2
Shell shape
Full size

Trapunto Corner Block
Template 3
Half shell shape
Full size

Trapunto Corner Block
Template 1
Full size

Trapunto Corner Block
Template 5
Full size

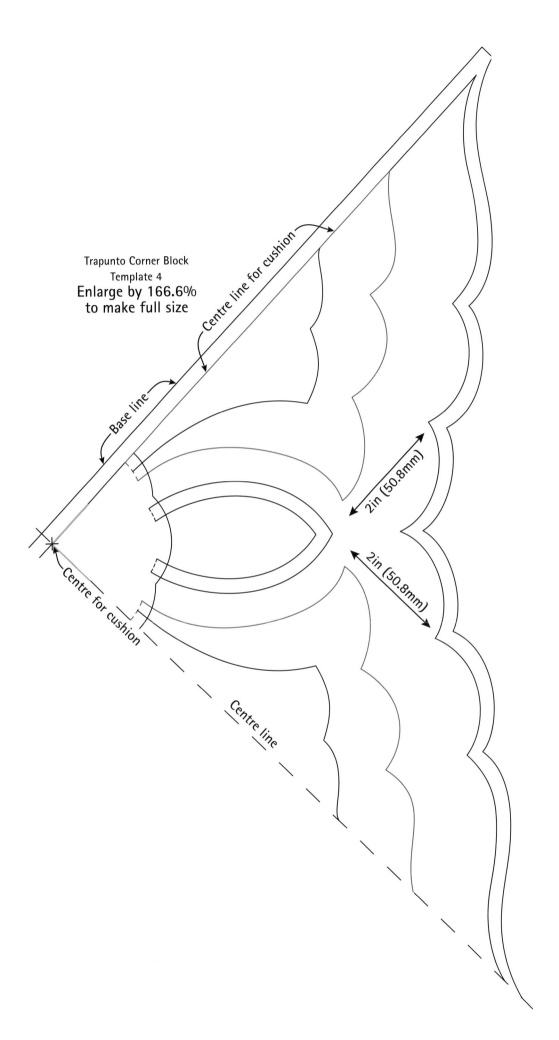

Trapunto Corner Block
Template 4
**Enlarge by 166.6%
to make full size**

Centre line for cushion

Base line

Centre for cushion

Centre line

2in (50.8mm)

2in (50.8mm)

Smocking Block

Many moons ago I hand smocked dresses for both of my daughters. Now I can do it on my machine in a fraction of the time although I don't think my girls would thank me for it! There are four Smocking blocks in the Heirloom Quilt and the instructions describe how to make one. To make four, quadruple the amounts in the You Will Need list. Before starting on the blocks you might want to practise your smocking skills by making the gorgeous Christmas Stocking on page 71.

you will need

(to make four blocks multiply the amounts given by four)

- Light shade of silk 5in x 36in (12.7cm x 91.5cm) strip, cut with long edge parallel to the selvedge
- Light shade of silk for corners 7in (17.8cm) square
- Fusible interfacing, one 5in x 13in (12.7cm x 33cm) strip and one 7in (17.8cm) square
- Tear-away stabilizer
- Wadding (batting) 9in (23cm) square
- Threads: 30 weight rayon thread for top and bobbin thread or polyester for bobbin
- Open toe or embroidery foot
- Smocking pleater (optional)
- Air-erasable marker

Finished size of block: 8¹⁄₁₆in (20.4cm) square, includes ½in (1.3cm) seam allowance for quilt assembly

Techniques: smocking by machine (page 135) • decorative stitching (page 106) • triple stitch (page 109)

Pleating/Gathering and Decorating the Strip

1 If you own a smocking pleater then use this to pleat the fabric strip. However, these are not easy to come by and are quite expensive but you can gather the fabric on your sewing machine – refer to Smocking by Machine on page 135.

2 Pull up the bobbin threads and adjust the strip to measure 13in (33cm) long. If you used a pleater, then adjust the pleats to the same length.

3 Iron the 5in x 13in (12.7cm x 33cm) strip of fusible interfacing to the wrong side of the strip to secure the gathers/pleats.

4 Using an air-erasable marker, draw a line down the centre of the strip. Beginning on this line, decorate the band with embroidery stitches, making the final decorated panel no more than 3in (7.6cm) wide. Trim the panel to 4in (10.2cm) wide.

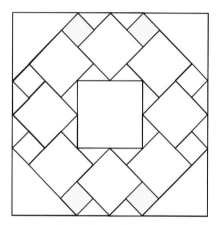

Position of the four Smocking blocks in the Heirloom Quilt

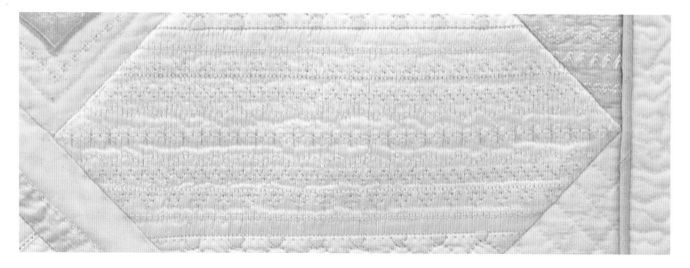

Sewing the Triangles to the Smocked Panel

5 Fuse the interfacing to the silk square and cut it diagonally. Sew the diagonal edge of a triangle to each long edge of the smocking panel using ¼in (6mm) seams.

6 Draw a 1in (2.5cm) grid on the triangles as follows. Using an air-erasable pen or similar, mark the centre of the seam that joins the smocking and the triangle at each side. Using the same pen, mark every 1in (2.5cm) along the seam, beginning from the centre and going towards each side. Draw lines from these marks to the opposite edge of the square and parallel to the other side of the square (Fig 1). Next, draw lines from the marks in the opposite direction (Fig 2).

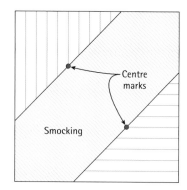

Fig 1

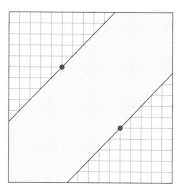

Fig 2

7 Pin the wadding to the back of the square. Sew a triple straight stitch, length 3, on the marked grid lines using a rayon 30 weight thread in the top and 50 weight in the bobbin. Sew the same stitch between the lines, forming a ½in (1.3cm) grid. Place tear-away stabilizer underneath and rip off each time before sewing the next line.

8 Either stitch in the ditch of the two diagonal seams on the square, or sew a buttonhole appliqué stitch with the claws going on to the triangles and the straight stitch in the ditch on the smocking side.

9 At each point where the triple stitch lines of the grid meet the diagonal seam, sew a single decorative stitch or bead. Cut the square to 8¹/₁₆in (20.4cm). Your Smocking block is now finished: go on to make three more. See page 76 for the next quilt block.

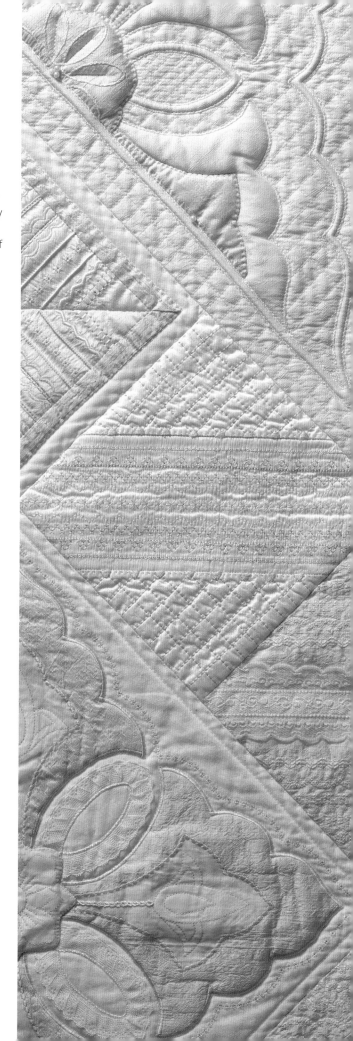

Smocked Christmas Stocking

A gorgeous Christmas stocking is a lovely project to show off your machine smocking skills and makes a wonderful gift for a loved one. I chose a red satin for the stocking but any festive colour would do – try gold, emerald or sapphire. I used gold 'glittery' fabric for the top band.

Finished size of stocking: 15in (38cm) long x 10in (25.4cm) wide (38cm long x 25.5cm wide)
Techniques: smocking by machine (page 135) • decorative stitching (page 106) • making and applying piping (page 141)

Making the Smocked Insert

1 Pleat or gather the 6in x 36in (15cm x 91.5cm) strip, referring to Smocking by Machine on page 135. Adjust the strip to measure approximately 8in (20cm) long and even out the pleats/gathers.

2 Iron the fusible interfacing to the back of the strip. Using an air-erasable or similar marking pen, draw a line down the centre of the strip and then a line either side of the centre, 1¼in (3.2cm) away.

3 Decorate the strip with decorative embroidery stitches, beginning at the centre line and ending the rows on or near the outer lines (see Smocking by Machine).

Inserting the Piping

4 On the right side of the smocked panel, draw a line 1½in (3.8cm) either side of the centre. Cut the piping into two equal lengths. Pin a piping strip, one on each line, to the right side of the smocked panel so that the stitching line on the piping is directly on top of the drawn line. The stitching line on the piping is in the ridge where the cord meets the tape. The tape of the piping should be facing away from the decorative stitches (Fig 1). Machine tack (baste) in place.

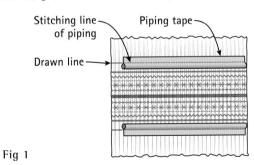

Stitching line of piping — Piping tape —
Drawn line —

Fig 1

5 Cut out the front and back stocking pieces using Template 1 on page 74 – the template will need to be enlarged by 200% to make it full size. Make sure that the front and back pieces will both face the same way when sewn. Draw a line on the right side of the smocked panel, ½in (1.3cm) from one of the piping stitching lines. With right sides together, pin the top of the shorter stocking piece to the smocked panel, sandwiching the piping and matching the raw edge with the line you just drew. Machine sew ½in (1.3cm) from the raw edge i.e., next to the piping that is between the two layers (Fig 2).

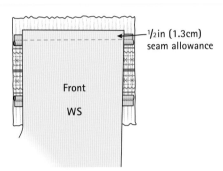

½in (1.3cm) seam allowance

Front
WS

Fig 2

6 Trim the excess pleated/gathered fabric to the raw edge of the stocking in the seam allowance (Fig 3). Open out flat and press the seam allowances towards the foot of the stocking.

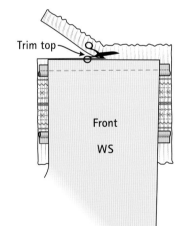

Trim top —

Front
WS

Fig 3

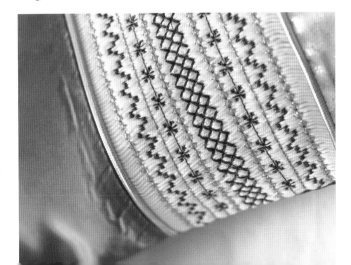

71

Attaching the Back and Top Band

7 With right sides together, pin the stocking pieces together. Trim the top of the back stocking piece at the top edge if it extends beyond the edge of the piping tape that is underneath.

8 Trim the excess smocked panel at the sides, level with the edges of the back stocking (Fig 4). Leave the excess at the top as this will remain to give the band more support.

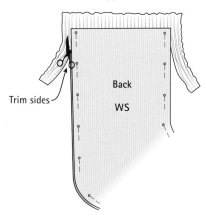

Trim sides

Back

WS

Fig 4

9 Using either seam/overlock stitch or straight stitch and a ¼in (6mm) seam, begin at the top of the toe side of the stocking and sew all the way around, stopping just below the smocked panel on the heel side (Fig 5). Turn the stocking right side out.

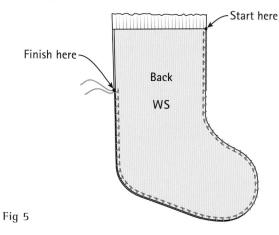

Start here

Finish here

Back

WS

Fig 5

10 Fold the band strip in half lengthways. Beginning at the opening, pin the band all the way around the top edge of the stocking. Place right sides together and align the two raw edges of the band strip with the edge of the piping tape on the front (Fig 6) and with

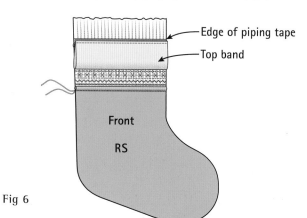

Edge of piping tape

Top band

Front

RS

Fig 6

the raw edge at the top of the back of the stocking (Fig 7). Machine in place using a piping or zipper foot for the front and changing to a regular foot for the back, keeping the seam allowances the same width.

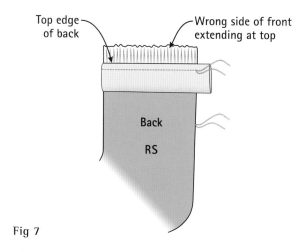

Top edge of back

Wrong side of front extending at top

Back

RS

Fig 7

11 Turn the stocking through to the wrong side. Draw a line on the pleated/gathered fabric that extends at the top, just a little less than half the depth of the band from the sewing line to the fold. Cut on the line (Fig 8).

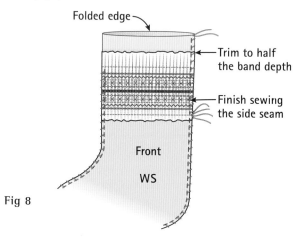

Folded edge

Trim to half the band depth

Finish sewing the side seam

Front

WS

Fig 8

12 Finish sewing the side seam to the top of the band. Cut off any excess band fabric at the sides. Fold the band in half to the inside of the stocking over the pleated/gathered fabric and hand sew the folded edge to the stocking on the inside to finish (Fig 9).

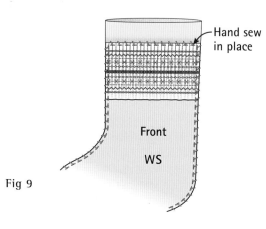

Hand sew in place

Front

WS

Fig 9

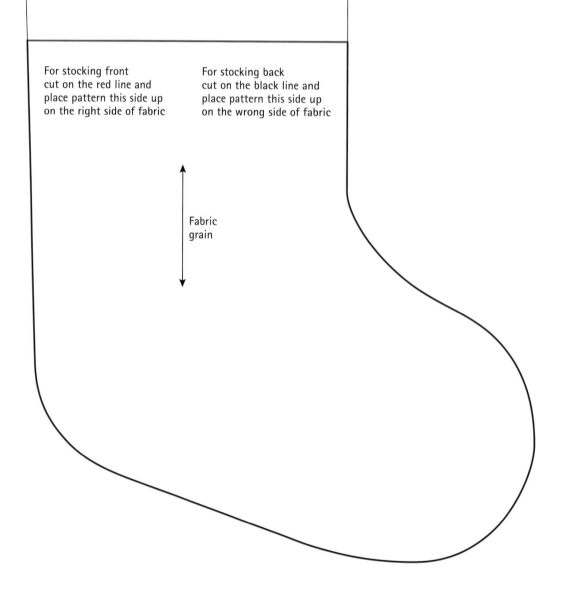

Smocked Christmas Stocking
Template 1
Enlarge by 200% to full size

For stocking front
cut on the red line and
place pattern this side up
on the right side of fabric

For stocking back
cut on the black line and
place pattern this side up
on the wrong side of fabric

Fabric
grain

Corded Wavy Tucks Block

The Corded Wavy Tucks block in the Heirloom Quilt is very pretty, with the wavy tucks corded and then anchored with tiny pearl beads. The two centre rows of tucks form a cathedral window effect. The instructions describe how to make one block. To make four, quadruple the requirements in the You Will Need list. The template on page 81 will need to be enlarged to full size – see instructions.

Finished size of block: 8¹⁄₁₆in (20.4cm) square, includes ½in (1.3cm) seam allowance for quilt assembly
Techniques: corded wavy tucks (page 137) • cathedral windows (page 139)

Sewing the Tucks

1 Cut out two shapes from the light shade silk using Template 1 on page 81. Enlarge the template by 200% to make it full size. Make sure the fabric grain line is parallel to either the straight or crosswise grain – not the bias grain.

2 With right sides facing, tack (baste) the two shapes together 1in (2.5cm) from the long straight edge. Iron the seam open.

3 With the wrong side up on the ironing board, use a hera marker or something similar to mark three lines 1½in (3.8cm) apart from either side of the centre seam. Fold the fabric on each line and iron the three creases either side of the centre, wrong sides together (Fig 1).

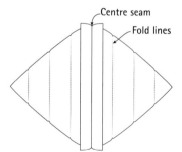

Centre seam
Fold lines

Fig 1

4 Keeping the pleats folded, sew a straight stitch ¼in (6mm) away from each folded edge. Make sure your thread matches the fabric as closely as possible on the top and in the bobbin. Refer to page 137 Corded Wavy Tucks.

5 Now sew ¼in (6mm) either side of the centre seam. Iron the tucks away from the centre.

6 Cut the square of fusible interfacing in half diagonally and place the two triangles on the back of each square, tucking the diagonal edge under the seam allowance. Iron them in place.

you will need
(to make four blocks multiply the amounts given by four)
- Light shade of silk 20in (51cm) square (or 18in x 44in (46cm x 112cm) for four blocks)
- Dark silk in a contrasting shade one strip 2in x 14in (5cm x 35cm)
- Fusible interfacing 9in (23cm) square
- Wadding (batting) 9in (23cm) square
- Decorative cord such as rayon bouclé 3½yd (3m) – see Suppliers
- Fifty tiny beads approximately
- Decorative braid or lace 15in (38cm) x ³⁄₈in (1cm) wide (optional)
- Machine feet: quarter inch foot and an edge-joining or ditch quilting foot (optional)
- Threads: machine sewing thread to match fabric and rayon machine embroidery thread to match cord
- Tear-away stabilizer

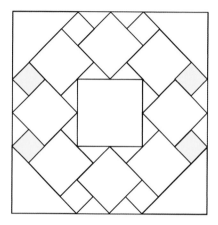

Position of the four Corded Wavy Tucks blocks in the Heirloom Quilt

Inserting the Window Decoration

7 Place tear-away stabilizer behind the 2in x 14in (5cm x 35.5cm) strip of dark shade or contrasting silk and either sew a decorative stitch or a decorative braid or lace on the right side down the centre.

8 Place the strip, right side up, centrally under the centre seam of the tucked shapes. Roll the seam over the top of the strip to make sure it's running along the centre. Pin the strip either side of the centre. To keep the strip in place tack (baste) approximately ½in (1.3cm) either side of the seam.

Completing the Wavy Tucks

9 Refer to Corded Wavy Tucks on page 137 to sew the cord to the folded edges. Remove the tacking (basting) from the centre seam and sew cord to both seam edges. Place a 9in (23cm) square of wadding (batting) underneath the shape.

10 To form the undulating or wave-like tucks continue as the technique on page 137 without sewing the centre edges to the background at this stage.

Manipulating the Windows

11 Sew the centre seam edges together at the marked points that are in line with the tucks that are pointing towards the centre seam (see step 4, page 139 Cathedral Windows).

12 Fold back the centre seam edges between each sewn point away from the centre and sew the edges to the background as before. These points will be in line with the tucks that are facing away from the centre seam (see step 5 Cathedral Windows) Remove the tacking (basting) stitches either side of the centre seam.

13 Sew beads to each sewn point through all layers or if you prefer, sew one decorative stitch at each point. Do not sew any beads further out than a 7in (18cm) square because they will be in the way when the blocks are assembled. Your Corded Wavy Tucks block is now finished: go on to make three more. See page 82 for the next quilt block.

Wavy Windows Bag

The course I run on making this stylish bag, which has a manipulated inset, has been very popular with my ladies, who say they receive many compliments when using it. It is not only striking but the zip placket along the top makes it look very professional. One lady made seventeen bags to give as Christmas presents!

Finished size of bag: 12in (30.5cm) x 12in (30.5cm) x 3½in (9cm)
Techniques: corded wavy tucks (page 137) • cathedral windows (page 139)

Making the Inset

1 Place the two strips of contrasting fabric for the wavy tucks, right sides together with the lighter shade on top. Position a long ruler on top of the fabrics so that the edge runs from one corner and along the bias grain (Fig 1). Using an air-erasable marker or similar, draw a line along the top edge of the ruler on to the fabric.

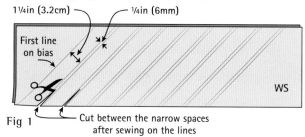

Fig 1

2 Draw a second line 1¼in (3.2cm) from the first and then another ¼in (6mm) from the second one. Repeat this seven times.

3 Using a lightning stitch or small zigzag (length 1.0, width 1.0), machine down the lines. Both stitches will stretch a little, enabling you to fold back the finished edge for the wavy tucks. Cut the strips apart between the narrow spaces. Turn each strip through to the right side and press with an iron. You should have eight strips each about 1in (2.5cm) wide. Cut each strip 11in (28cm) long.

4 Lay the inset background on top of the interfacing. Draw a line ½in (1.3cm) in from each 11in (28cm) edge. Pin the strips across the background with the outside edge of the first and last ones next to the lines. Machine tack (baste) the strips to the background along the top and bottom.

5 Using an air-erasable marker, draw a line on the strips ½in (1.3cm) from the top edge and another one ½in (1.3cm) from the bottom edge. Sew a triple stitch or zigzag stitch, length 0, on the lines at each point where the edges of the strips meet to join them together and anchor them to the background. Sew the same stitch on the side edges to the background of the first and last strip.

you will need
For the bag:
- Fabric for two front sides each 11in x 2½in (28cm x 6.5cm)
- Fabric for one front top strip 13in x 2in (33cm x 5cm)
- Fabric for one front bottom strip 13in x 3¾in (33cm x 9.5cm)
- Fabric for one back 13in x 14¾in (33cm x 37.5cm)
- Fabric for two sides each 12in x 4½in (30.5cm x 11.4cm)
- Two zip plackets each 13in x 3½in (33cm x 9cm)
- Two zip placket facings each 13in x 2½in (33cm x 6.5cm)
- Two straps each 30in x 3in (76cm x 7.5cm)

For the inset panel:
- Fabric for the background 10in x 11in (25.5cm x 28cm)
- Heavyweight interfacing 10in x 11in (25.5cm x 28cm)
- Two strips of contrasting fabric for the wavy tucks each 9in x 28in (23cm x 71cm)

For the bag lining:
- Fabric for front, back and base 13in x 27in (33cm x 68.5cm)
- Fabric for two sides each 12in x 4½in (30.5cm x 11.4cm)

Other materials:
- Two straps of heavy interfacing each 30in x 1in (76cm x 2.5cm)
- One base of thick card 11¾in x 3¼in (30cm x 8.2cm)
- Open-ended zip 14in (35.5cm) long
- Machine sewing thread to match your fabrics
- Air-erasable marker
- Edge-joining or ditch-stitching foot (optional)

6 Mark 2½in (6.3cm), 5in (12.7cm) and 7½in (19cm) from the top ½in (1.3cm) line along the edges of the strips and triple stitch or zigzag them together as before (Fig 2).

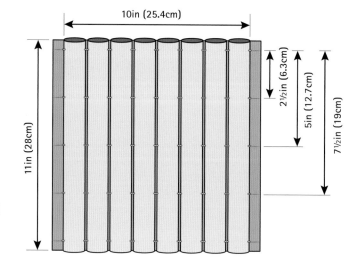

Fig 2

7 Bend back the edges of the strips between the stitching and then triple stitch or zigzag the edges together midway between the previous stitching (Fig 3).

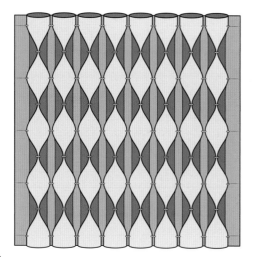

Fig 3

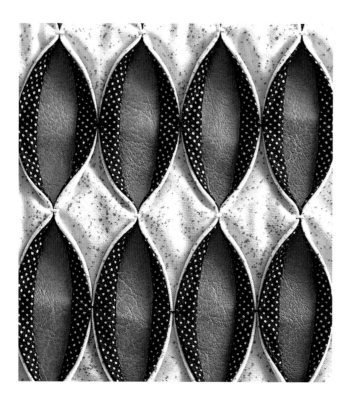

Making the Bag

8 All seams are ½in (1.3cm) and pieces are sewn right sides together unless otherwise stated. Sew the two side panels to the side edges of the inset. Open out the side panels and sew the front top strip and front bottom strip to the top and bottom edges of the inset.

9 Sew the bag back to the bag front along the bottom edge. Press the seam open. Topstitch either side of the seam about ¼in (6mm) away to keep the seam allowances flat.

10 With wrong sides together, fold the bag 1¾in (4.4cm) either side of the bottom seam and press with an iron. Keeping it folded, sew a line of straight stitching very close to the folded edges. This will form the base of the bag (Fig 4). Use a ditch-stitching or edge-joining foot if you have one, with the needle moved to the left a little. Guide the edge of the fold along the left of the centre guide on the foot and because the needle has been moved over, you will sew a perfectly straight line close to the edge.

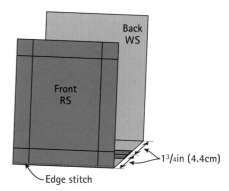

Fig 4

11 Turn over ½in (1.3cm) to the wrong side at the top of both side panels and press with an iron.

12 Sew the bottom edge of the sides to the side edges at the base of the bag. Begin and end the seam ½in (1.3cm) in from the ends and line up the seam at the base of the bag with the centre of the strip. Mark 1½in (3.8cm) from the top of the front and back at each side edge.

13 Clip into the stitching at the base of the bag that joins the sides to the bag (Fig 5). Pivot the edge where it has been clipped and sew the side panels to the bag, ending with the fold at the top of the sides, level with the 1½in (3.8cm) marks at the top of the bag sides. Edge stitch along the sides as you did in step 10.

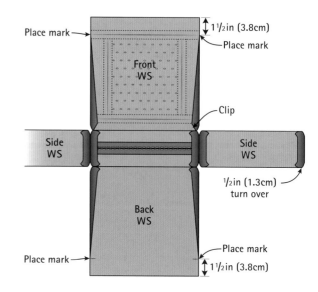

Fig 5

14 To make the straps, on the wrong side mark a line 1in (2.5cm) from one long edge. Fold the raw edge to the line giving a ½in (1.3cm) turning. Place the interfacing strip on the wrong side of the strap down the centre. Turn the raw edge over to the top of the interfacing and then bring the folded edge over to cover the raw edge. Pin and sew a decorative stitch from the front down the centre to secure. Tack (baste) the ends of one strap to the front of the bag and the other to the back along the top of the bag, 3in (7.6cm) in from the sides.

Inserting the Zip

15 At the short ends of the zip plackets and the zip placket facings, fold over ½in (1.3cm) to the wrong side. Pin each zipper tape between a placket and zip placket facing, with the right side of the zip facing the right side of the placket. The raw edges should be even with the edge of the tape, with the teeth on the zip facing in. The bottom end of the zip will extend. Sew in place using a zipper foot (Fig 6). Turn the facing and placket to the right side and topstitch through all layers close to the zip teeth. Turn both tapes at the top end of the zip between the facing and placket and edge stitch the folded side edges of the placket and facing together.

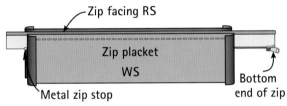

Zip facing RS

Zip placket

WS

Metal zip stop

Bottom end of zip

Fig 6

16 Sew the top of the bag front to the lower edge of the placket and then the top edge of the back to the lower edge of the other placket. There will be ½in (1.3cm) seam allowance extending at either end. Fold this over to the inside and edge stitch in place.

Lining the Bag

17 Place the card base inside the bag at the bottom. On the wrong side, mark the middle of both long sides of the lining and join the marks with a crease. Draw a line 1¾in (4.4cm) either side of the crease. Fold right sides together along the lines and edge stitch along the folds. This will form the base of the lining, as you did for the bag.

18 Turn over ½in (1.3cm) to the wrong side at the top of both lining side pieces. Sew these to the sides of the bag lining as you did for the bag, ending 1in (2.5cm) from the top of the front and back edges. Place the lining inside the bag, wrong sides together. Pin the top folded edges of the lining and bag sides together and edge stitch.

19 On the back, fold the zip placket against the top of the bag, wrong sides together along the seam that encases the straps. Place the raw edge of the back lining between the zip facing and the bag back. With the bag still folded over at the top, sew a line of stitching 1in (2.5cm) from the top of the bag back through all layers to encase the lining.

20 Repeat step 19 for the bag front. The 1in (2.5cm) stitching line at the end will be along the seam at the top of the inset on the front. Your bag is now finished.

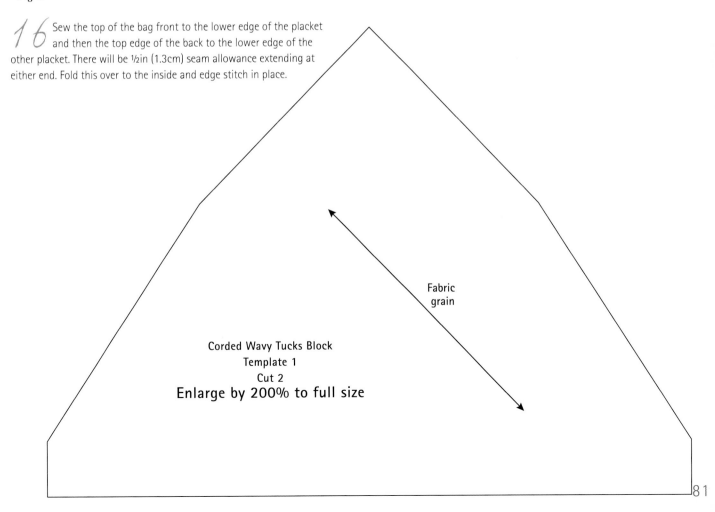

Fabric grain

Corded Wavy Tucks Block
Template 1
Cut 2
Enlarge by 200% to full size

Lace and Twin Needle Block

This block is perfect for learning how to make your own lace on the sewing machine and how to use a twin needle to transform the look of your decorative stitches. Eight of these attractive triangular blocks are needed for the Heirloom Quilt. The directions are for making one of them. To make eight, multiply the requirements in the You Will Need list by eight.

Finished size of block: 8¹³/₁₆in (22.4cm) square cut in half diagonally, includes ½in (1.3cm) seam allowance for quilt assembly
Techniques: machine lace (page 121) • decorative twin needle sewing (page 128)

you will need
(to make eight blocks multiply the amounts given by eight)
- Bridal tulle or organza 8½in x 3in (21.6cm x 7.6cm)
- Water-soluble stabilizer two strips each 8½in x 3in (21.5cm x 7.6cm) (see step 1)
- Dark shade of silk, half a 10in (25.4cm) square cut diagonally
- Fusible interfacing half a 10in (25.4cm) square cut diagonally
- Wadding (batting) half a 10in (25.4cm) square cut diagonally
- Threads: 40 weight rayon machine embroidery thread (one for the lace and one to contrast with the silk) and bobbin thread
- Twin needle 2.0mm
- Tear-away stabilizer
- Air-erasable marker
- Open-toe foot

Making the Lace

1 Refer to Machine Lace on page 121 to sew the lace strip using either organza or fine net (bridal tulle). The finished size should be approximately 8½in (21.6cm) long x 2in (5cm) wide.

Sewing the Twin Needle Stitches

2 Refer first to Decorative Twin Needle Sewing on page 128. Iron the interfacing to the wrong side of the silk triangle. Using an air-erasable marker, draw a line down the centre of the silk on the right side from the point at the top to the raw edge at the base. Draw a line 1½in (3.8cm) away from either side of the centre (Fig 1). Draw another line ½in (1.3cm) above the raw edge at the base of the triangle.

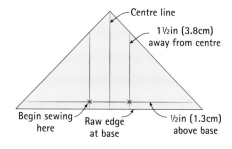

Centre line
1½in (3.8cm) away from centre
Begin sewing here
Raw edge at base
½in (1.3cm) above base

Fig 1

3 Place tear-away stabilizer under the triangles and a 2.0mm twin needle in your machine. Use two reels of rayon embroidery thread in the top and bobbin or polyester thread in the bobbin. All machines either have an extra spindle built in at the top of the machine or one that can be inserted – refer to your instruction manual for threading a twin needle. Attach the open-toe or embroidery foot. The line above the raw edge at the base is the seam line. Begin the first row of stitches at the seam line – you will be sewing towards the pointed end. By starting here, when the triangles are sewn in place, you will have complete stitch patterns starting at the seam. This will work well if any of the patterns are mirror imaged for the opposite side.

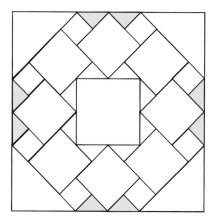

Position of the eight Lace and Twin Needle blocks in the Heirloom Quilt

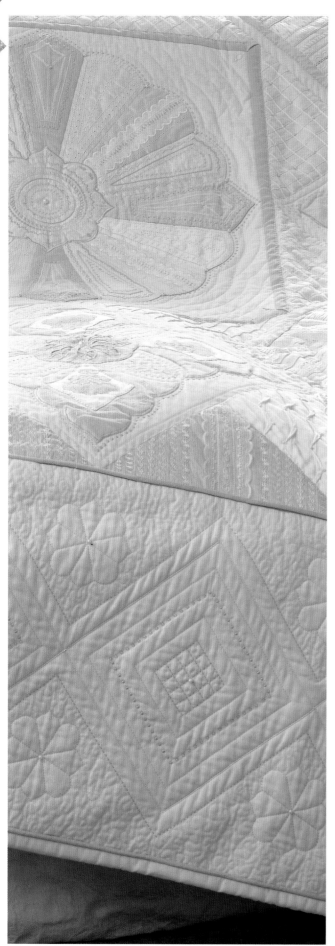

4 Select a stitch pattern that you have practised beforehand and begin with the needle on the point where the line at the side of the centre and the line above the base intersect. Sew towards the pointed end of the triangle and press the 'Pattern End' or 'Stop' button, if your machine has one, to complete the stitch. By doing this you will be starting at the beginning of the stitch pattern for the next row. Carefully tear away the stabilizer. Mirror image the stitch pattern if needed, replace the stabilizer and sew down the other side of the centre on the line.

5 Continue in this manner sewing rows of twin needle stitches, guiding the edge of the presser foot along the edge or centre of the previous row of stitches.

Attaching the Lace

6 Place the lace strip on the triangle so that the top of a scallop is on the base line and the centre row of stitches is over the centre line of the triangle. Use a straight stitch, length 2.5, and thread to match the stitching on the lace. Sew down the lines of stitching either side of the centre stitches. If this is a row of entredeux stitches, the needle should go into the holes at every stitch – with a little care and some manoeuvring!

7 Place the wadding (batting) centrally under the triangle and pin down the centre through all layers. To attach the wadding to the silk, proceed as follows. Fold back the lace edge on the left-hand side of the centre on top of itself. Attach the zipper foot so the needle is on the right side of the foot. Using a thread to match the silk, sew a straight stitch, length 2.5, right next to the row of straight stitching that is securing the lace to the silk. Change the zipper foot so the needle is on the left of the foot and repeat for the other side of the lace (Fig 2).

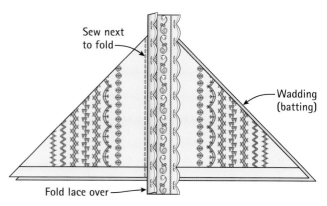

Sew next to fold

Wadding (batting)

Fold lace over

Fig 2

8 Cut the triangle to a diagonal half of an 8¹³/₁₆in (22.4cm) square. Your Lace and Twin Needle block is now finished: go on to make seven more. See overleaf for the next quilt block.

The techniques of lace making and twin needle sewing can be used to decorate many items, such as this nightdress shown here. For an extra special gift, make the cutwork box on page 52 to hold the present.

Crosshatched Block

These easy little crosshatched triangles surround the Dresden Plate in the Heirloom Quilt and the pin-tucking technique can be used on many projects where a textured fabric is required – you could use it for a bag for example. These instructions are for making two of the triangular blocks and the materials listed are also sufficient for two blocks. To make eight, multiply the requirements by four.

Finished size of block: 8¹³/₁₆in (22.4cm) square cut in half diagonally, includes ½in (1.3cm) seam allowance for quilt assembly
Techniques: crosshatching (page 130)

Sewing the Pin-Tucks

1 Place your fabric wrong side up and along the top edge draw a small mark 1½in (3.8cm) from the left edge and another 1½in (3.8cm) from the right edge. Beginning from the mark on the left, draw marks ¾in (1.9cm) apart all the way along the top edge with the last one ¾in (1.9cm) from the mark at the right. Repeat for the opposite edge (the one along the bottom).

2 Place the square on an ironing board or similar soft surface, wrong side up, and using a hera marker or similar make a crease joining each pair of opposite marks (see page 130 Crosshatching).

3 Edge stitch the folds using the same thread in the top and bobbin that is the closest match to your background. Iron the square lightly on the right side of the fabric so the tucks lie in the same direction before ironing flat from the wrong side.

4 Now repeat steps 1, 2 and 3 to make tucks going in the opposite direction.

Finishing the Block

5 Iron the square of fusible interfacing to the wrong side of the crosshatched square and then pin the square of wadding (batting) underneath. Machine tack (baste) the layers together, about 1in (2.5cm) from the edges.

tip

To machine tack (baste), select a straight stitch adjusted to length 4.0–6.0 and loosen the top tension a little (lower number). If your machine has a tension dial set to Auto, this usually means the default tension is around 4.0, so turn it to 3.0 to loosen it slightly.

you will need
(sufficient for two triangles – to make eight blocks multiply the amounts given by four)
- Medium shade of silk or calico 11¼in (28.5cm) square
- Fusible interfacing 10in (25.4cm) square
- Wadding (batting) 10in (25.4cm) square
- Twenty tiny beads (optional)
- Thread to match fabric
- Edge-joining foot or ditch-stitching foot (optional)

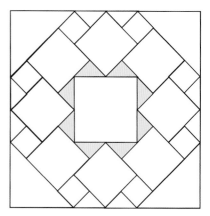

Position of the eight Crosshatched blocks in the Heirloom Quilt

6 Draw a diagonal line across the square, which should ideally go through where the pin-tucks intersect. Using a walking foot, machine tack (baste) on the diagonal line.

7 Sew a decorative stitch or a tiny bead at alternate junctions of the tucks through all layers (see Fig 1). Trim the square to 8¹³/₁₆in (22.4cm) and then cut it on the diagonal that has been machine tacked (basted) to create two triangular blocks. Go on to make three more sets of Crosshatched blocks. Your Heirloom Quilt is now ready for assembly, borders and finishing.

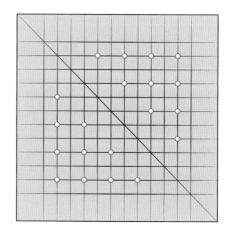

Fig 1

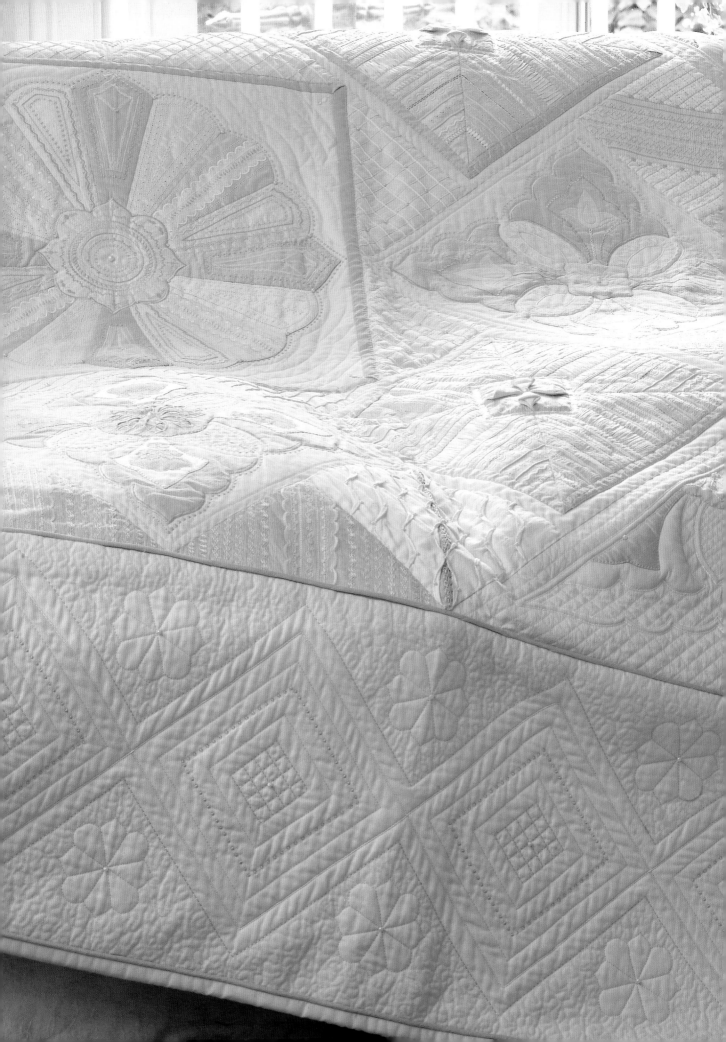

Making up the quilt

Joining the Quilt Blocks

All your blocks are made – well done! It's time now to sew them all together. Use a ½in (1.3cm) seam allowance throughout and make sure that you are accurate with this, otherwise it will cause problems. If you don't have a ½in (1.3cm) guide mark on your stitch plate see the tip below for advice. When the blocks have been joined, the backing fabric is attached and quilted to the top. The borders are then made and sewn to the quilt and finally the edge is bound.

Finished size of quilt top: 61in x 61in (155cm x 155cm), includes ½in (1.3cm) seam allowances
Finished size of completed quilt: 90in x 90in (228.6cm x 228.6cm)
Techniques: machine quilting (page 131) • echo quilting (page 133) • making and applying piping (page 141)

you will need

- Fabric for the quilt back 64in x 64in (162.5cm x 162.5cm)
- Dark shade of silk for border around the Dresden Plate block 90in x 1in (228.6cm x 2.5cm) (shorter lengths can be joined with a diagonal seam)
- Bias tape maker ½in (1.3cm) (optional)
- Machine sewing thread for quilting
- Hand tacking (basting) thread
- Safety pins
- Walking foot
- Machine quilting or size 80 needle

tip

If you don't have a ½in (1.3cm) guide mark on your stitch plate, stick a strip of masking tape to the plate so the edge is ½in (1.3cm) away from the needle. Another method is to draw a line on a piece of paper ½in away from the edge. Place the paper under the foot so the edge of the paper is either level with the right-hand edge of the foot or with one of the marks on the stitch plate – usually the 10mm line. Move the needle until it is on top of the ½in (1.3cm) line you drew. Remove the paper and the needle will be in the correct position when the edges of the fabric are lined up with the mark on the stitch plate or edge of the foot.

Joining the Blocks around the Dresden Plate

1 Trim ½in (1.3cm) of the wadding (batting) from each edge of all the blocks where possible. Trim another ¼in (6mm) of wadding from each point or corner of all the blocks.

2 On the right side of each of the two Cutwork blocks and the two Shadow Appliqué blocks, mark the ½in (1.3cm) seam line at one corner. Next mark the centre of the two sides that meet at the marked corner (Fig 1).

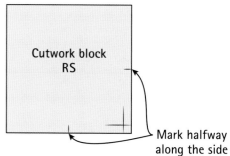

Fig 1

Cutwork block
RS

Mark halfway along the side

3 Cut each of the four Crosshatched blocks along the diagonal line that has been machine tacked (basted), if you haven't already done so. Trim ½in (1.3cm) of the wadding from this edge – you should have already trimmed the wadding from the other two sides of the triangle. Trim another ¼in (6mm) of wadding from each corner. Mark the ½in (1.3cm) seam line on the back of the triangles on all sides.

4 Pin a triangle to one of the marked sides of the squares, right sides together. The point where the seam lines meet at the right-angled corner on the triangle should match the centre mark of the side of the square, marked A on Fig 2. The point where the seam lines intersect at the point of the triangle should match with the point where the seam lines intersect at the corner of the block, marked B.

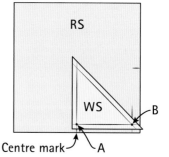

RS

WS

B

Fig 2   Centre mark   A

5 Sew a ½in (1.3cm) seam beginning approximately 1in (2.5cm) from the centre mark at the side of each square and ending at the ½in (1.3cm) mark at the corner (Fig 3).

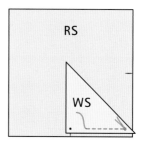

RS

WS

Fig 3

6 Repeat steps 4 and 5 for the adjoining side of the square that has been marked and another triangle (Fig 4). Iron seams open and fold the points flat at the corners.

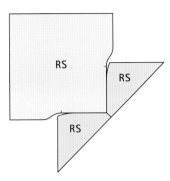

Fig 4

7 Attach all of the eight triangles in this way, two to each of the Cutwork blocks and two to each of the Shadow Appliqué blocks.

8 On the front of the Dresden Plate block, mark the ½in (1.3cm) seam line at each corner. Next mark the centre of each side. With right sides together, pin the diagonal sides of the two adjoining triangles that are sewn to one of the Cutwork blocks to one of the sides of the Dresden Plate block. Match the centres and the points where the seam lines intersect at the corners. Sew together with ½in (1.3cm) seam beginning and ending at the ½in (1.3cm) seam mark at the corners (Fig 5).

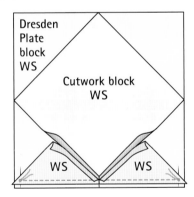

Fig 5

9 Pin and sew the other Cutwork block and triangles to the opposite side of the Dresden Plate block in the same way. Press open both seams.

tip

Skipped stitches are most often caused because the wrong needle is being used, especially when sewing microfibre or a closely woven fabric, where a microtex sharp needle would be best as it will pierce the fibres. A quilting needle is required when sewing with wadding (batting), a stretch needle for stretch fabrics and a metallic needle for metallic threads. Skipped stitches can also occur when sewing over chalk markings.

10 Pin and sew the two Shadow Appliqué blocks with the triangles attached to the remaining two sides of the Dresden Plate in the same way. Iron the two seams open (Fig 6).

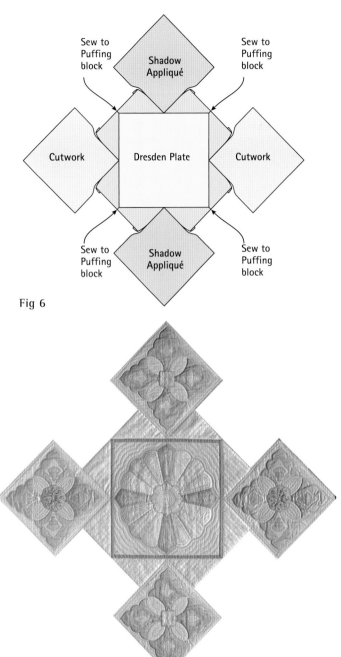

Fig 6

11 On the right side of each of the four Puffing blocks, mark the seam line at each corner and the centre of each side as before.

12 With right sides together, pin one side of each Puffing block to each pair of triangles, matching the centre of the side of each block with a corner of the Dresden Plate where the triangles meet. Sew a ½in (1.3cm) seam all the way across, beginning at one end and ending at the other. Press the seam open.

13 Repeat step 12 for the remaining Puffing blocks. Hand sew all the seam allowances over the wadding to keep them in place.

Joining the Remaining Blocks

14 On the wrong sides, mark the ½in (1.3cm) seam allowances at each corner of the four Smocking blocks and the four Corded Wavy Tucks blocks.

15 Mark the three corners and centres of the remaining two sides of the Cutwork and the Shadow Appliqué blocks as before.

16 With right sides together, pin one side of a Smocking block to a side of a Shadow Appliqué block at the end where it will join the Puffing block. Match the centre mark on the side of the Shadow Appliqué block with the ½in (1.3cm) mark at one corner of the Smocking square. Match the corners at the other end of the two blocks. Sew a ½in (1.3cm) seam beginning approximately 1in (2.5cm) from the centre mark and finishing at the end at the corner (Fig 7).

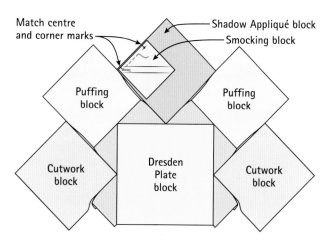

Fig 7

17 Pin and sew another Smocking block to the other edge of the same Shadow Appliqué block in the same way and then sew the two remaining Smocking blocks to the other Shadow Appliqué block. Before you sew these, check that when the Smocking blocks are flipped to the right side, one edge will be next to the Puffing block and that the seam is at right angles to it (Fig 8).

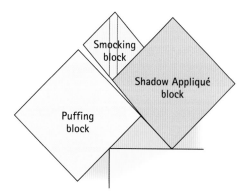

Fig 8

18 Sew the four Corded Wavy Tucks blocks to the Cutwork blocks in the same way, following Fig 9.

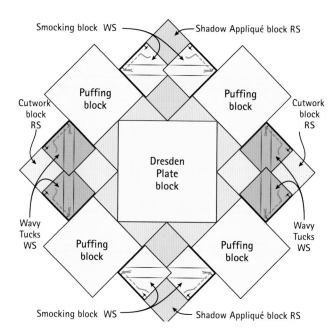

Fig 9

19 Press all seams open and hand sew the seam allowances over the wadding as before. With right sides together, sew one side of each Puffing block to the Shadow Appliqué and Smocking blocks and the other side to the Cutwork and Corded Wavy Tucks blocks, all the way along. Iron the seams open and sew down the seam allowances over the wadding.

20 With right sides together, sew a Lace and Twin Needle triangle to each of the Smocking and Corded Wavy Tucks blocks, matching the corners and midpoints as before (Fig 10). Press the seams open and then sew the other side of the triangle to the Shadow Appliqué and Cutwork blocks, all the way along. The diagonal edge of the Lace and Twin Needle triangles will be next to the border of the quilt.

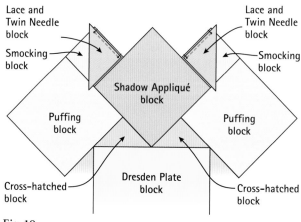

Fig 10

21 Press the seams open. With right sides together, pin the diagonal edge of each Trapunto block to each corner of the quilt along the edge of the Smocking, Puffing and Corded Wavy Tucks blocks (Fig 11). Sew a ½in (1.3cm) seam all the way across. (A few of my ladies panicked at this stage when they mistakenly tried to sew the Trapunto blocks to the Lace and Twin needle blocks and found they didn't fit!) Press seams open and hand sew seam allowances as before.

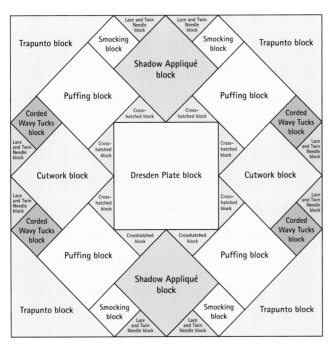

Fig 11

Backing and Quilting

22 Lay the quilt top, right side down on a large table. If you don't have a table large enough for the whole quilt, then work on one half at a time. Pat the quilt so there are no wrinkles. Carefully place the backing fabric, right side up on top of the quilt, making sure that the backing covers all the outside edges of the quilt top. (The backing is larger and will be trimmed to the correct size before attaching the borders.) Starting in the centre, pat the backing to eliminate any wrinkles – do not scrub it with the palms of your hands as this will stretch the fabric and cause wrinkles on the front of the quilt. Beginning at the centre, tack (baste) the layers together by hand. Avoid tacking on top of the seams if you can. Your tacking rows should be approximately 6in (15cm) apart and go in both directions in a grid pattern.

23 Turn the quilt over and place safety pins through all layers across the seam lines about every 8in (20.3cm). Tacking and pinning this much is quite time consuming but will make the quilting process easier.

24 Using a walking foot and your choice of thread, stitch in the seam ditches beginning at the centre of the quilt and working towards the edges. I used the bridging stitch for the seam ditches – see page 131 Machine Quilting for more information.

25 Plan what other areas you are going to quilt and complete the areas that can be sewn with a walking foot first. You can quilt as much or as little as you like. The larger bocks will need to be quilted more than just along the outside seam to prevent the layers sagging if the quilt is hung. There is no need to quilt the smaller shapes. When you have finished with the walking foot, either use the free-motion foot (see page 134 Free-Motion Stippling) or a regular sewing foot to sew the other areas if you need to – these will be the more curvy shapes. I have listed below where I quilted, but feel free to decide for yourself where and how you quilt.

Dresden Plate block: quilted around the edge of the centre, between the petals in the seam ditch and around the outside edge of the petals. Echo quilting between the outside edge of petals and the edge of the block (see page 133 Echo Quilting). Sew the same border of silk strip you used around the Puffing block over the seam on the outside of the Dresden Plate block if desired.

Puffing blocks: quilted around the centre square, the four diagonal seam ditches from the corner of the centre square to the corner of the edge of the border tape and around the outside edge of the tape.

Cutwork and Shadow Appliqué blocks: quilted around the centre, around the large shells and ½in (1.3cm) in from the outside edge of the finished square.

Trapunto Corner blocks: quilted around the half circle, around the large shells and around the outside edge of the Italian quilting.

Once all quilting is finished you can move on to adding the borders and finishing the quilt.

Adding Borders and Finishing

The borders for the Heirloom Quilt are quilted and cut to size before they are sewn to the quilt. This means that you don't have to manipulate a large quilt under the machine, which makes life a lot easier! The background stippling is optional and has to be done after the borders are sewn to the quilt. Nearly all of the ladies in my classes who have made the quilt decided not to add the stippling and the result is just as good. There are four borders and four corners in the Heirloom Quilt and the instructions in this section are for making one border and one corner but the You Will Need list below includes the requirements for making all four borders and corners. Templates are given on pages 98–99 – see the instructions there for enlarging templates 2, 3, 4 and 5.

Finished size of border: 61in x 15½in (155cm x 39.5cm) which includes ½in (1.3cm) seam allowances
Finished size of corner: 15½in x 15½in (39.4cm x 39.4cm) which includes ½in (1.3cm) seam allowances
Techniques: machine quilting (page 131) • couching (page 111) candlewicking by machine (page 113) • triple stitch (page 109) making and applying piping (page 141) • double-fold binding with mitred corners (page 141)

you will need

(to make four borders and four corners)
- Four pieces of calico or silk for border front 64in x 15½in (162.5cm x 39.4cm)
- Four pieces of calico for border back 64in x 15½in (162.5cm x 39.4cm)
- Four pieces of calico for corner front 15½in x 15½in (39.4cm x 39.4cm)
- Four pieces of calico for corner back 15½in x 15½in (39.4cm x 39.4cm)
- Four pieces of wadding (batting) 64in x 15½in (162.5cm x 39.4cm) plus four squares 15½in x 15½in (39.4cm x 39.4cm)
- Fine cord for couching 26yd (24m) approximately
- Threads: machine sewing thread for quilting – I used 30 weight rayon – and thread for the bobbin (this will show on the back of the quilt border)
- Machine quilting needle
- Walking foot and narrow braid/cording foot (optional)
- Template plastic
- Erasable fabric marker

To finish the quilt:
- Piping cord 4mm thick, four 62in (160cm) lengths and four 92in (234cm)
- Dark shade of silk for the piping, four 62in (158cm) and four 92in (234cm) lengths of 2in (5cm) wide (can be made up of shorter lengths joined with diagonal seams)
- Calico or silk for binding 3¼in (8.3cm) wide strips to total 10½yd (9.8m) (can be shorter lengths joined with diagonal seams)
- Fifty small beads (3mm–4mm diameter)

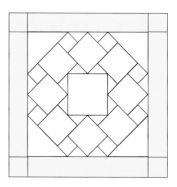

Position of the borders in the Heirloom Quilt

Marking the Border Top

When the blocks of the quilt are sewn together it should measure 61in (155cm) across the centre from raw edge to raw edge in both directions. The borders are quilted before they are sewn to the quilt top which means that as the fabric puckers a little you will have a slightly shorter length than when you started. To compensate for this, you will need to mark the borders ¾in (2cm) longer than the quilt measurement and make a final adjustment before attaching the borders to the quilt.

1 Using template plastic, draw and then cut out one of each of the following five squares: 7³⁄₁₆in (18.2cm), 5¾in (14.6cm), 4½in (11.4cm), 3¼in (8.2cm) and 2in (5cm).

2 Finger press a crease horizontally and vertically down the centre of the border top in both directions. On the horizontal centre crease line, beginning at the centre point, mark every 10⅛in (25.8cm) to the left and the same to the right. You will have about 1½in (3.8cm) remaining at each end.

3 Position the 7³⁄₁₆in (18.2cm) square template diagonally along the border centre crease line between the first two marks. Each of the marks should be at a corner of the template. Draw a mark on the border top at each of the two other corners of the template. Move the template and repeat for the remaining marks. Using a ruler and suitable removable fabric marker join the marks to form six squares positioned diagonally along the border top (see Fig 1). These are the lines for the couched cord.

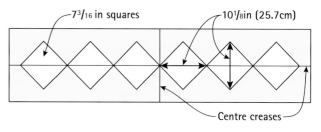

Fig 1

4 Mark the centre of each square and the centres of each of the remaining squares you cut from the template plastic. To mark the centre of a square, join both pairs of opposite corners with a straight line. Where they intersect is the centre of the square.

5 Draw around each of the remaining template squares on to the border top so they are centred in each of the larger squares (Fig 2).

Fig 2

Layering and Quilting the Borders

6 Layer the wadding (batting) between the wrong side of the border top and wrong side of the border back. With the right side of the border top facing up, pin and then machine tack (baste) the layers together. Using a walking foot, sew a line from the centre out in both directions, a line between each large square from top to bottom edges and then a line around the edges, again working from the centre out.

7 Thread your machine with your chosen thread and begin by sewing a straight stitch, length 3.0 around each of the 3¼in (8.2cm) and 5¾in (14.6cm) squares you marked on the border top (Fig 3).

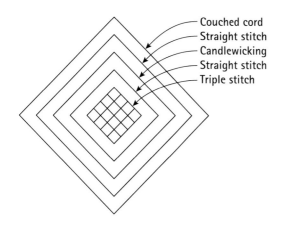

- Couched cord
- Straight stitch
- Candlewicking
- Straight stitch
- Triple stitch

Fig 3

8 Sew a triple stitch (or straight stitch) around each of the 2in (5cm) squares (see page 109 Triple Stitch). Sew a candlewicking stitch (see page 113 Candlewicking by Machine) or similar around each of the 4½in (11.4cm) squares.

9 To couch the cord around the 7³⁄₁₆in (18.2cm) square, use either a cording/braiding foot or walking foot and begin at one end, leaving a 2in (5cm) tail (see page 111 for Couching). Attach the cord in a zigzagged line along the sides of the squares across to the other end, secure the threads and cut the cord off, leaving a 2in (5cm) tail (Fig 4). Begin again and sew across to the opposite end in the same way. The

reason for cutting the cord off and starting again at the end rather than continuing around the corner is that you may need to adjust the point where the cord meets before sewing the border to the quilt.

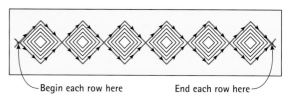

Begin each row here   End each row here

Fig 4

tip

If you are able to, buy a braiding guide for your machine, this will be really useful as the cord is fed through it, leaving both hands free to guide the fabric.

10 Draw a line ⅝in (1.6cm) from the sides of the 7³⁄₁₆in (18.2cm) squares (the ones you couched the cord along) and sew a triple stitch (or straight stitch) along this line. Draw a ½in (1.3cm) grid inside each of the 2in (5cm) squares and sew a triple stitch (or straight stitch) on the lines.

11 Draw around the small flower shape in Template 1 overleaf (it is given full size), placing it in the triangle between each outer square, with the top 2¼in (5.7cm) below the point where the couching lines intersect. Sew around each shape and the inner lines with a straight stitch.

Marking the Corners

12 On the right side of the square for the corner front, draw a line across the two diagonals with a suitable fabric marker. Now use Templates 2, 3, 4, 5 and 6 overleaf: templates 2, 3, 4 and 5 need to be enlarged by 125% to full size; template 6 is given full size and needs to be drawn and then flipped vertically and drawn again to create the whole shape. Using the templates draw the shapes on to the corner front, placing them centrally each time and with the points of the shaped templates pointing towards the corners of the square.

Layering and Quilting the Corners

13 On each of the four corners, layer the wadding square between the wrong side of the corner top and wrong side of the corner back. With the right side of the corner top facing up, pin and then machine baste the layers together using a walking foot.

14 There are five shapes to sew around for each corner, stitched as follows.

a) Inner circle – triple stitch (or zigzag stitch).

b) Next circle – straight stitch.

c) First flower shape – candlewicking stitch or similar (use the 'Stop' or 'Pattern End' function for sewing around the curves).

d) Second flower shape – couched cord.

e) Outer flower shape – straight stitch.

Finish by sewing a ½in (1.3cm) grid in triple stitch (or straight stitch) inside each inner circle (grid lines are shown on Template 2).

Completing the Borders

15 Measure the borders between where the couched cord around the 7³/₁₆in (18.2cm) square intersects at either end. This should be the width of your quilt, measured across the middle, minus 1in (2.5cm) for the seam allowances. If this measurement isn't the same, you can either reposition the cord ends or simply end the borders at the same measurement as the quilt. Mark both ends of the borders at this measurement from the top to the bottom – this will be the stitching line. Draw a line ½in (1.3cm) away from these marks for the seam allowance (Fig 5). Cut the borders along these lines at both ends through all thicknesses. Before you cut, check to make sure that the measurement between the two cutting lines on the borders is the same measurement as the width of the quilt top from raw edge to raw edge measured across the middle.

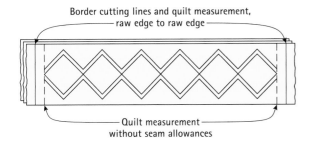

Border cutting lines and quilt measurement, raw edge to raw edge

Quilt measurement without seam allowances

Fig 5

16 With right sides together, pin the *top layers only* of the corner squares, one to each end, to two of the borders. Sew the two layers together with a ½in (1.3cm) seam. Press the seam allowances open. On the back, trim the wadding so the edges that are over the seam butt together. Hand sew the two edges together with a herringbone stitch or similar. Fold under the seam allowance of the border backing and pin this over the seam allowance of the corner backing. Slip stitch in place along the fold (Fig 6).

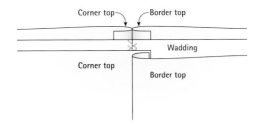

Corner top   Border top

Wadding

Corner top

Border top

Fig 6

Attaching the Piping and Borders

17 Trim the backing of the quilt level with the edges of the quilt top. Refer to page 141 Making and Applying Piping and sew the prepared piping in place, trimmed to ½in (1.3cm) seam allowance, one strip to each side of the quilt top.

18 Trim the wadding ½in (1.3cm) from one long edge of each border strip. This will be the edge that is sewn to the quilt. On the wrong side of a border with no corner attached, pin back the wadding and backing fabric away from the edge where you trimmed the wadding, leaving the top border layer free. With right sides together, pin the top layer of the border to all thicknesses on one side edge of the quilt top. Make sure you match the ends and midpoints before sewing in place with a ½in (1.3cm) seam allowance. Use a piping or zipper foot for this as the ridge of the piping is under the top layer. On the back, turn under the seam allowance of the border backing and slip stitch in place. Repeat for the other border without the corner and the opposite side of the quilt.

19 Attach the borders with the corners in the same way, sewing the corners to the ends of the borders that are already attached. If you want to stipple quilt the border, do it at this point – see page 134 Free-Motion Stippling.

Finishing the Quilt

20 All that is left is to apply more piping and then bind the quilt edges. For the requirements see the You Will Need list on page 94. Start by tacking (basting) the edges of the quilt ¼in (6mm) from the edge using a walking foot.

21 Refer to page 141 Making and Applying Piping and sew the prepared piping, trimmed to ½in (1.3cm) seam allowance, one strip to each side of the quilt top.

22 To prepare and sew the binding, follow the instructions on page 141 for Double-Fold Binding with Mitred Corners. Lastly, don't forget to sew a label to the back of your quilt (see page 142). Sit back and admire your work – your Heirloom Quilt is now finished!

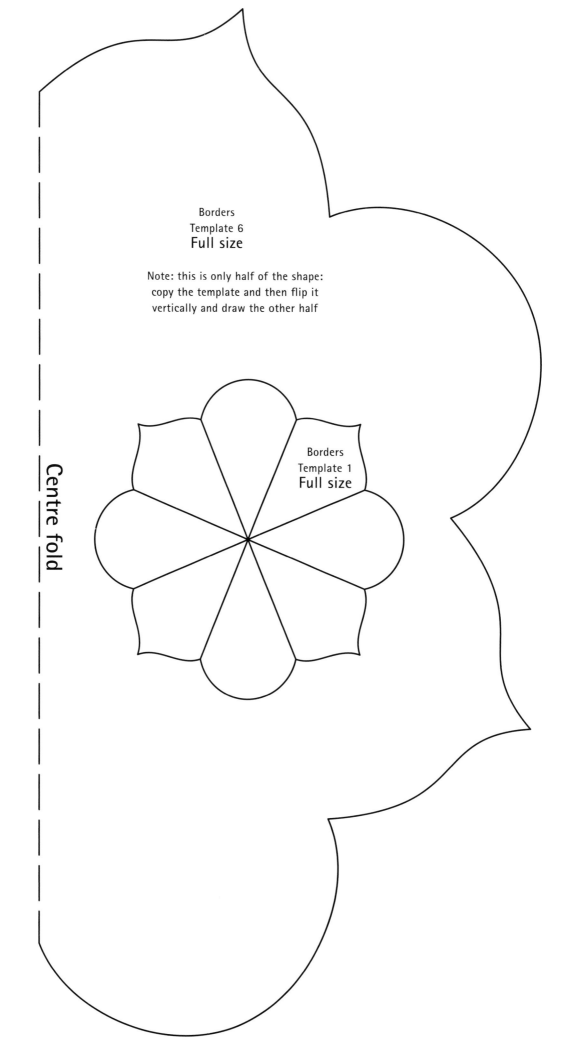

Borders
Template 6
Full size

Note: this is only half of the shape:
copy the template and then flip it
vertically and draw the other half

Borders
Template 1
Full size

Centre fold

Corner Templates
Enlarge Templates 2, 3, 4 and 5 by125% to full size

Template 5

Template 4

Template 2

Template 3

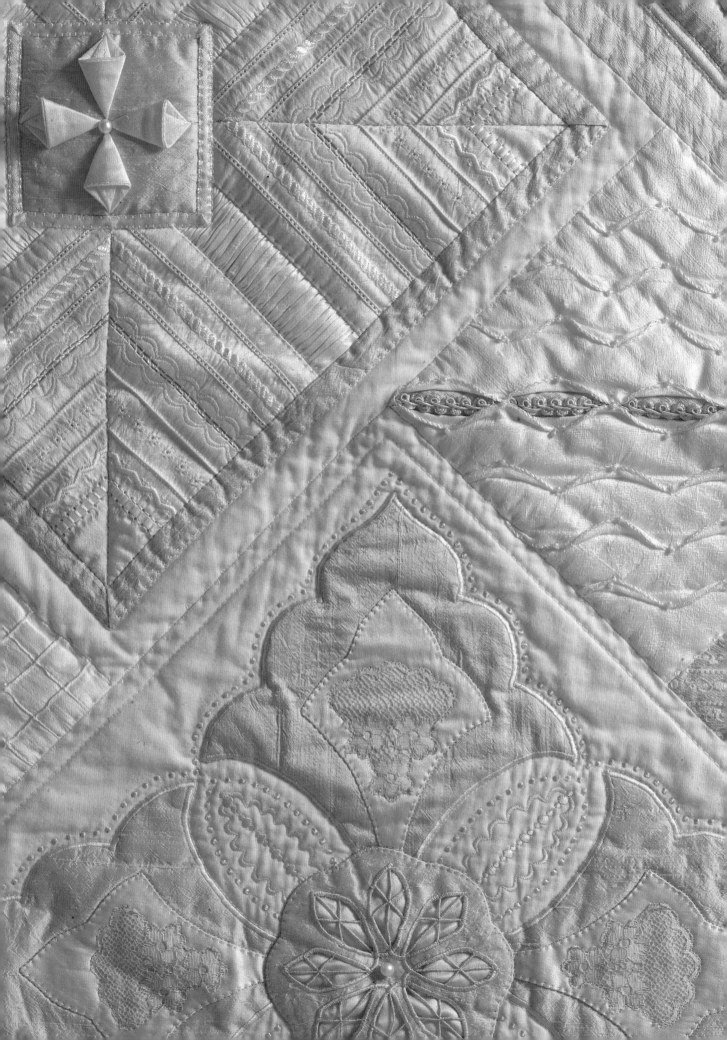

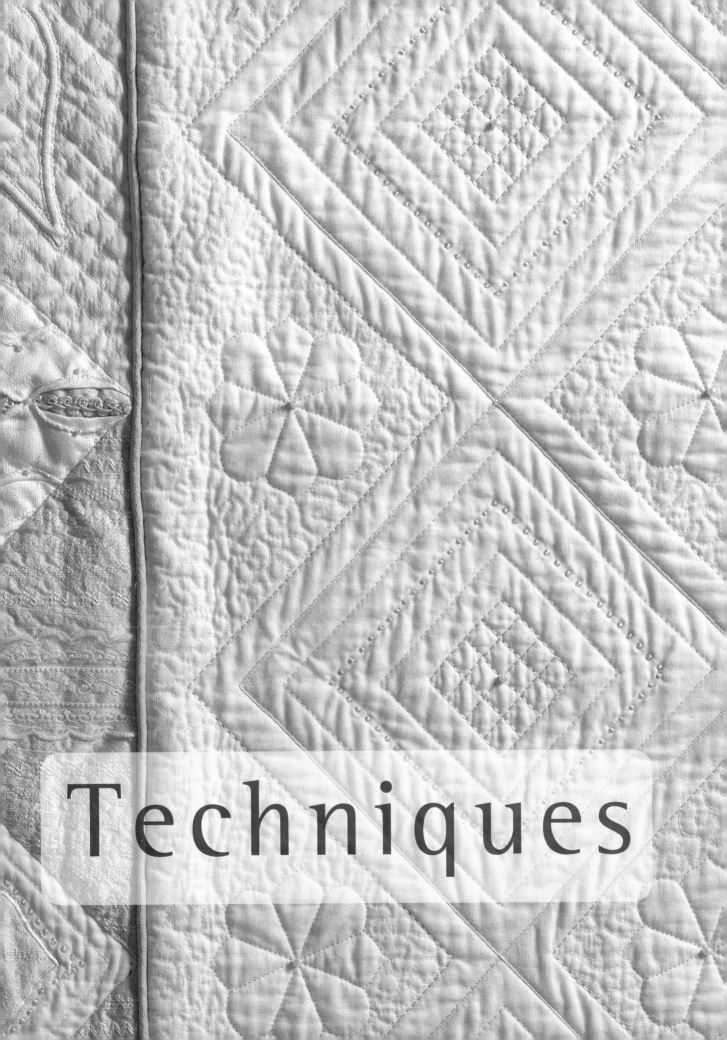

Techniques

Techniques

All of the techniques you will need to make the Heirloom Quilt and the smaller projects in this book are contained in this section, illustrated with diagrams and pictures where necessary. The techniques are also referenced in the Index.

Using Your Sewing Machine

You will be surprised at how many of the techniques in this book can be done using just a basic sewing machine, many of them using just a straight or zigzag stitch. However, a machine with a selection of decorative stitches is preferable. If you own a more advanced, computerized machine then this book will teach you how to use it to its full potential.

If you are looking to upgrade your machine or buy your first one, the choice can be a little overwhelming. There are so many makes and models of sewing machine, each with different functions, stitches, accessories and prices, that it is sometimes difficult to choose which one to buy. Bear in mind the following points.

- Consider what you will be using the machine for – is it going to be mainly for dressmaking, patchwork and quilting, creative machine sewing, free machine sewing or embroidery?
- If you are a dressmaker, you will probably want to try out the buttonhole facility. A quilter may want to try the walking foot and free-motion facility. For creative machine sewing, try out the wing needle stitches, satin stitch, triple stitch, buttonhole appliqué stitch and some of the decorative stitches.
- Go along to your dealer with some samples of the types of fabric you will be using and try these out on the machines in your price range.

Machine Functions

Each machine has different functions, and usually the more there are, the more expensive the machine! The following is a list of some of the functions you will find used on different makes of machine. I have marked those that I think are the most important for creative machine sewing with an asterisk. It is a good idea to take some time to look at your sewing machine manual and identify these functions.

- Length and width adjustment *
- Needle stop up/down *
- Mirror image (sideways) *
- Stop/pattern end *
- Fix/secure/locking stitch
- Mirror image (top to bottom/end to end)
- Variable speed
- Start/stop (to use without the foot pedal)
- Stitch re-start
- Stitch density control/elongation
- Stitch positioning
- Reverse

Can My Machine Sew the Heirloom Quilt?

The short answer to this is yes – if your machine can make a zigzag stitch with a length adjustment this will mean that you can sew a satin stitch. Even an inexpensive machine can create some wonderful effects. True, there are some techniques featured in the Heirloom Quilt that look their best when done with more advanced machines but alternatives are offered throughout the book and the results you will achieve will still be wonderful. The following points should help, as will taking the time to read your sewing machine manual.

- Twin needle sewing – all sewing machines that have a swing needle (that is, can do a zigzag stitch) can take a twin needle. Machines either have an extra spindle built in at the top of the machine or one that can be inserted – refer to your instruction manual for threading for a twin needle.
- Triple stitch – this may be one of your basic stretch stitches, so double check to see if you have this. If not, then use a straight stitch instead.

- Candlewicking – if you aren't able to programme this or it's not a built-in stitch then select a small decorative stitch, or a simple stretch zigzag and adjust the length and width so that it is quite small and dainty. Alternatively, this stitch can be omitted and you will still have a lovely heirloom quilt!
- Chain stitching – your machine will be able to do this because all that is needed is a straight stitch.
- Couching and sewing over cord – you only need a zigzag stitch for this.
- Wing needle – a zigzag stitch will work for wing needle sewing but a stretch zigzag and some other stretch stitches would be better still.
- Finished-edge appliqué – instead of using a buttonhole appliqué stitch for this you could use a blind hem stitch or even a zigzag.
- Circular sewing – a few decorative stitches would be lovely, however, you could alternate the rows between straight or triple stitches and zigzag or stretch zigzag stitches.
- Pulled thread sewing – this technique uses a triple stitch or straight stitch.

- Shadow appliqué – this just uses a normal straight stitch.
- Lace shaping – this technique uses a straight stitch and/or zigzag.
- Sewing lace motifs – use a straight stitch or zigzag stitch for this technique.
- Machine lace – you really need some decorative stitches for this but if you don't have any, then you can always cheat a little and add a length of purchased lace!
- Cutwork – this only uses straight stitch, zigzag and satin stitch.
- Puffing and crosshatching – straight stitch is all that is needed for these techniques.
- Italian quilting and trapunto – straight stitch is all that is needed for these techniques.
- Faggoting – a zigzag stitch would suffice for this technique, although a stretch zigzag would be even better.
- Corded wavy tucks and cathedral windows – straight stitch and zigzag are all that are required.
- Piping, binding and finishing the quilt – only straight stitch is needed for these techniques.

Accessory Feet

A sewing machine will include a number of accessory feet, which you will need to take into consideration when comparing prices. Some may include a walking foot. It is important to use the correct foot for the job – a straight stitch foot for instance will wobble over satin stitching, whereas an embroidery foot or open-toe foot will remain flat because it has a groove underneath for the thickness of the stitch to sit in. The quickest way to figure out which foot to use is to turn it over so you can see the width and thickness of the grooves, especially for the different sizes of piping feet, braiding feet and pin-tucking feet (see examples below). The following is a list of the different feet I've used in the book, with suggestions in brackets for alternatives you might use.

- Candlewicking foot (or use an embroidery, open-toe foot or walking foot).
- Edge-joining foot, ditch-stitching foot and narrow-edge foot (or use a standard stitching foot or open-toe foot).
- Five-groove pin-tuck foot (or use an embroidery, narrow braiding foot, open-toe or three-groove cording foot, supplied with most Janome machines).
- Gathering foot (or use an embroidery foot, with the tension adjusted to a higher number).
- Narrow braid foot (or use a pin-tucking foot or embroidery foot).
- Open-toe foot (or embroidery foot).
- Piping foot (or use a zipper foot, beading foot, embroidery foot or walking foot).
- Seven-hole/nine-hole cording foot (or use an open-toe foot, twin needle foot or three-groove cording foot, supplied with most Janome machines).
- Spanish hemstitching foot/faggoting/bridging guide (or use a strip of template plastic or plastic coffee stirrer – see Faggoting page 126).
- Stippling foot (or use a darning foot).
- Walking foot, dual-feed/even-feed foot (or an embroidery foot).

A selection of sewing machine feet

gathering foot

seven-hole cording foot

three-groove cording foot

open toe feet

seven-groove pin-tucking foot

edge-joining or ditch-stitching foot

five-groove pin-tucking foot

narrow edge foot

Stitch Length

On most makes of machines, the stitch length of a decorative pattern refers to the length in millimetres of *each individual stitch* that makes up the pattern (Fig 1). This is sometimes referred to as the stitch density and is how I have instructed in this book. However, on some of the more recent machines, the length refers to the length in millimetres of *one stitch pattern* (Fig 2).

Fig 1   Fig 2

Machine Sewing – Troubleshooting Tips

Faulty stitching – If your stitching isn't looking good, first check that the bobbin thread isn't pulling through to the top. If so, this could be that either the top thread is caught somewhere (usually around the spool) or that the bobbin thread has come out of the tension guide. Make sure the needle is inserted properly and that you are using the correct foot. Sometimes when a machine jams, it will pull the top thread out of the tension discs and/or out of the take-up lever, so check this after you fix the reason for it jamming in the first place!

Thread breakage – If the thread breaks, especially metallic thread, this could either be that the wrong needle is being used or that the thread is twisting too much as it comes off the spool. Try placing the spool vertically if possible. This means that the spool turns to release the thread, rather than the thread twisting off when in the horizontal position. Occasionally, the thread will come off the reel too quickly, especially with a new reel. To overcome this try placing the reel flat on its base on the table behind your machine. Bring the thread up and over the back of the machine and into the first tension guide and then continue threading as normal.

Thread knotting – If the thread knots at the beginning of your stitching, get into the habit of holding the top thread down before the needle goes down into the fabric for the first stitch. If this fails, turn the machine off, clean out the raceway (the bobbin area), have a cup of tea and start again!

Irregular feeding – It is extremely important to keep the raceway or bobbin area clean and free from fluff, as not doing so can prevent the feed teeth/dogs from moving. I have known a machine to sew backwards because the bobbin area was so clogged. Consult your machine manual for instructions on cleaning this area. Other causes for irregular feeding could be a blunt needle, the wrong foot pressure and/or not enough stabilizer being used.

Continuous Sewing

Continuous sewing, sometimes referred to as chain sewing, saves time and thread when you are sewing multiple short lengths. This method is very useful if you are using cords or ribbon as you don't have to keep cutting them and re-threading or placing them under the presser foot.

At the end of your first row of stitching stop just beyond the edge of the fabric and leave it in the machine. Lift the presser foot and place the next piece of fabric to be sewn underneath the foot. Lower the presser foot and sew the next row. Continue like this until you have sewn all your pieces. Remove this long chain of fabric from the machine and then cut the threads that are joining the strips.

Chain Stitching

This technique is used in the Dresden Plate block, the nine-patch cushion and the Shadow Appliqué block. Chain stitching creates an attractive raised surface and is a useful technique in machine embroidery. The main steps are as described below.

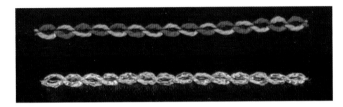

1. Cut a length of cord three times the length of the line to be sewn. Fold the cord in half to mark the centre and open out straight. Use an open-toe foot and set your machine to stop with the needle in the down position if you can.

2. Secure the cord centre at the top of the line using a stretch straight stitch or triple stitch, selecting the 'Stop' or 'Pattern End' button if you have one to make sure you sew only one triple stitch (see Fig 1). If you don't have a triple stitch, use a straight stitch, making sure you secure the threads at the beginning.

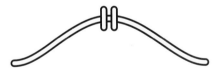

Fig 1

3. Sew one straight stitch (length 2.5) and stop with the needle in the fabric (see Fig 2 and the first photo, right). Lift the presser foot and cross the two lengths of cord over in front of the needle, bringing the cord ends towards the back (see Fig 3 and the second photo). Don't pull them too tightly. Lower the presser foot.

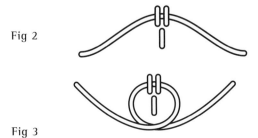

Fig 2

Fig 3

4. Sew two straight stitches and stop with the needle in the fabric. Lift the presser foot and cross the cord in front of needle. Lower the presser foot. Repeat this step all the way down, trying to keep the cord chain tension even (Fig 4).

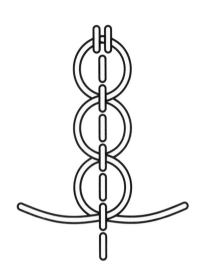

Fig 4

5. Stop just before the end of the line. Fix to secure the stitching and cut off the cord ends, leaving about 1½in (3.8cm) tails. Using a hand sewing needle with a large eye, pull the cord ends through to the back of the work.

When chain stitching with cord, after the first stitch stop with the needle in the fabric (first photo). Lift the foot, cross the cords over (second picture), lower the foot and sew two straight stitches. Continue on in this way.

Decorative Stitching

You may or may not have a wide selection of decorative stitches on your machine but even if you only have a few, the following tips will enable you to make them look their best.

Decorative Stitching Basics

- Use a stabilizer – using a tear-away stabilizer underneath the fabric you are sewing on is most important. There are many different makes of stabilizer. Some only tear easily in one direction so check this first as it is much easier to remove if it tears away easily in all directions. If you plan to sew more than one row of decorative stitches near each other and plan to remove the stabilizer, then tear it away after you sew each row. There are a couple of reasons for this. Firstly, it is much more difficult to tear off the stabilizer between rows of stitches as you can't get a good grip on it and end up tearing it off in tiny pieces. Secondly, the fabric may distort or pucker a little between the rows. This is easily rectified by simply slitting the stabilizer with a pair of scissors between the rows to release it or by tearing it away.

- Practise on scrap fabric – always have a few scraps of the same fabric that you will be sewing on next to your sewing machine and place a piece of tear-away stabilizer underneath each piece.

- Choose the right thread – rayon threads for sewing decorative stitches create a beautiful sheen and are available in two weights, 40 and 30. The thicker the thread, the lower the number, so a 30 weight thread is thicker than a 40 weight. I prefer using 30 weight threads as these are bolder and show up better although there aren't as many colour choices as the 40 weights. Use regular machine sewing thread (50 weight) in the bobbin or bobbin thread (60 or 70 weight).

- Use the right needle – there are many different types of machine needles, each designed for specific types of sewing, threads or fabrics. The size is given in metric and universal, i.e., 80/12 – the higher the number, the thicker the needle.

Embroidery needles are designed for machine embroidery using rayon threads and are therefore the best ones to use for decorative stitching. A size 75/11 is best for 40 weight threads and a size 80/12 for 30 weight threads. If you use a thicker needle for a close satin stitch it may make tiny holes in the fabric and weaken it.

- Select the right tension – a slightly looser top tension is required when sewing decorative stitches, especially if a satin stitch forms part or all of the pattern. With a slightly looser thread on the top you will have a more rounded, almost raised design and none of the bobbin thread showing at the sides. Machines with an automatic tension will adjust this when you select the stitch. If you do not have this function on your machine, turn the tension dial to a lower number. If the bobbin in your machine fits into a separate bobbin case that inserts under the stitch plate, it may have a tiny hole in the arm of the case. Pull the bobbin thread though the hole before you sew decorative stitches and buttonholes. This will slightly tighten the bobbin tension meaning that you may not need to loosen the top one as well.

- Decide on stitch length and width – before you sew any decorative pattern, play around with the length and width adjustments on your practice fabric as you may prefer the stitch to be shorter or longer than the default. When adjusting the length of satin stitched patterns, be aware that by making the pattern longer it will also open out the stitches. Similarly, by making it shorter the stitches will be closer together. Some machines have an 'elongation' function that will enable you to adjust the pattern length without altering the density, or keep the default pattern length and adjust the density of the stitches.

Left:
ideal tension
(top tension
loosened)

Right:
top tension
too tight

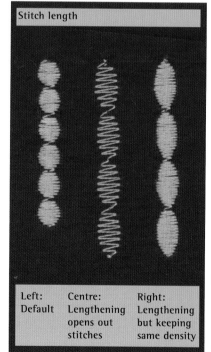

Stitch length

Left:
Default

Centre:
Lengthening
opens out
stitches

Right:
Lengthening
but keeping
same density

Starting a Row of Decorative Stitches

- Use a guide – before you sew a row of stitches you will need a guide to keep you on the straight and narrow, so either draw a line or use a guide. If you choose to draw a line, this can either be where the centre of the pattern will be sewn (in which case you will guide the centre of the foot down the line), or draw a line parallel with the edge of the foot and keep the foot edge along the line all the way down. Use an air-erasable or easily removable pen to draw the line. Instead of drawing a line as a guide you might use some of the following suggestions: press a crease in the fabric; guide the edge of the foot along the edge of a previous row of stitches; use a seam guide or guide the edge of the fabric along one of the marks on the stitch plate.
- Secure the starting stitch – the best results will be obtained by fixing the stitch at the beginning to secure the threads by either selecting the fix/secure function or by sewing a few tiny straight stitches on the spot. Many machines require that you hold down the top thread before the needle goes in for the first stitch. Not doing so could result in a clump of thread on the wrong side at the beginning so it's a good habit to get into. For satin stitched patterns (see Figs 1–4 below): after securing the threads, bring the top thread tail in front of the needle and sew over it for the first few stitches. Cut off the tail close to the stitches and continue sewing, trapping the very end of the thread. Hey presto, you won't have a tail to pull through to the back!

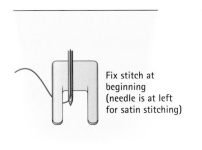

Fig 1

Fix stitch at beginning (needle is at left for satin stitching)

Fig 2

Bring thread end in front of needle

Fig 3

Sew satin stitch over thread end

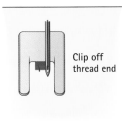

Fig 4

Clip off thread end

- Interrupted stitching – if for any reason you have to stop in the middle of a stitch pattern because the thread has broken or the machine has decided to throw a wobbly, then unpick the pattern back to the end of the previous stitch pattern and reset the stitch to start at the beginning, remembering to fix or secure the threads. Some machines have a re-start button that resets the stitch to begin at the start of the pattern, meaning you don't have to reset any length and width adjustments you may have made.

Programming Decorative Stitches

If your machine has a built-in memory that allows you to programme and save a sequence of stitches you will have to refer to the manual to do this as all makes and models of machines differ. However, there are some tips that apply to programming decorative stitches generally.

- When selecting a stitch design, look carefully at the needle position at the beginning and end of the pattern. The next stitch in your sequence will need to begin at the same position the previous one ended. A good example of this is a scallop design that starts and ends with the needle on the left. If you then mirror image the scallop for the next stitch in the sequence, the needle will move over to the right forming a jump stitch. Even if you select a different decorative stitch that begins with the needle in the centre, you will still have a jump stitch from left to centre where the two stitches meet.

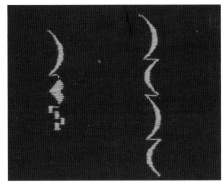

Jump stitches

- Sometimes there is a stitch design on your machine that is too close together, such as the daisy. You can overcome this by programming one design (a daisy) and then a straight stitch. However, if your machine enters more than one straight stitch at a time, you may be able to use the 'space' stitch, which is really one straight stitch (_ or □), sometimes found at the end of the alphabet menu. Consult your sewing machine manual for more on its functions.

Inserting a stitch between motifs

Turning Corners

Not all patterns work well at corners so play with your stitches on practice fabric to see which ones look good. When you reach a corner, stop with the needle in the fabric at the end of the stitch pattern. Some machines have a 'Pattern End' or 'Stop' function that will automatically do this when selected. Pivot and continue down the other side (see first picture below, top row). If you have a mirror image function on your machine, either side to side or top to bottom, or both, then you may be able to make a stitch work at a corner where it didn't work before – see first picture, second row. You could also try the following things.

- Mirror image the stitch side to side and/or top to bottom, before you begin to sew.
- Sew the stitch to the corner, pivot and mirror image side to side and/or top to bottom.
- Mirror image the stitch side to side and/or top to bottom at the beginning and take it off at the corner.

Note that the patterns in the lower sample are turned clockwise at the corner. If you will be turning the fabric anti-clockwise (counter clockwise) then you may have to mirror image the pattern side to side depending on its design. If you do not have a mirror image function on your machine you could begin at the bottom of the other side, turn clockwise at the corner and then sew along the top.

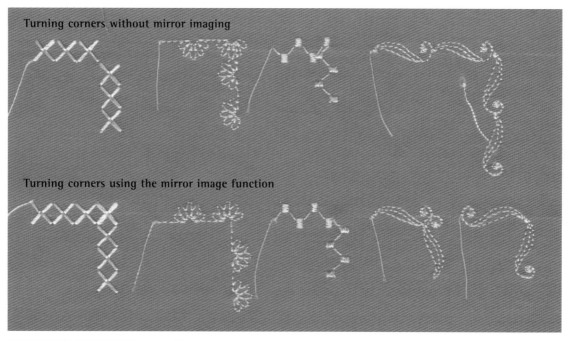

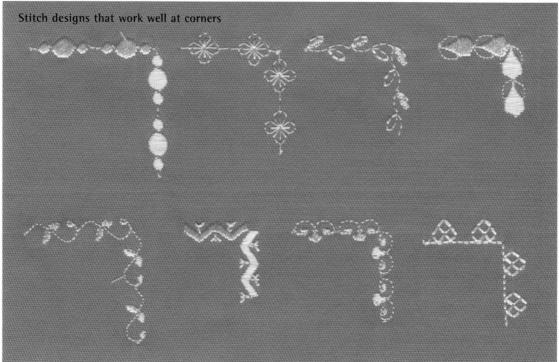

Triple Stitch

This is a straight stitch that goes forwards, backwards and forwards and is sometimes referred to as a straight stretch stitch or a reinforced straight stitch. On some machines it may go forwards, backwards and forwards twice.

The icon on your machine for triple stitch may look like one of those shown in Fig 1. I tend to use this stitch quite often for outlining designs as it gives quite a bold line, especially if with 30 weight thread.

Fig 1

You do, however need to be a little careful when sewing this stitch – these points should help.

- Don't hold the fabric too tightly. You need to allow the feed dogs to go backwards without any resistance otherwise the needle won't pierce in the same place and the stitches will look messy.
- When sewing curves, set your machine to stop with the needle down if possible and pivot only at the end of the stitch i.e., after it has gone forward, back and forward again. If you pivot halfway you will end up with a jagged line.
- For corners or points, again, pivot at the end of the stitch. Not doing so will result in a stitch sticking out from the point.

Sewing Over Cord

This technique is used in the Puffing block and the roll pillow project. Ideally, you will need to use a cording foot for this technique. These come in different shapes and sizes and are different from braiding feet as they have more than one hole and/or groove, allowing you to thread from three to seven strands of cord through. With a decorative stitch sewn on top of the cords, the result looks as though you have used a decorative braid, especially if you use different colours of cord or several strands of stranded cord. For the Puffing block, I used two lengths of stranded rayon cord threaded through the two holes in the middle row of a seven-hole cording foot. If you have a foot with three grooves, use three strands of cord.

1 Thread your chosen cords through the slots, grooves or holes in the cording foot and clip it on the machine. Choose a stitch pattern that has some open areas in it and adjust it to the widest setting – see Fig 1 for examples. Do not choose a solid satin stitch as this will cover too much of the cords. Avoid using stitches that have a long backward motion, otherwise the cords will get tangled.

Fig 1

2 Cut your cords long enough to sew at least one row and thread them through the presser foot. Hold the cords at the back of the presser foot before you begin sewing. Use a tear-away stabilizer underneath your fabric and sew slowly, keeping the cords straight as they feed into the front of the foot. Stop every few inches to straighten the cords. You may need to lengthen your stitch pattern a little because of the bulk of the cords, especially if you are using a pattern with some satin stitching.

3 At the end of the row of stitching, pull the cords an inch or so through the cording foot and cut them at the back of the foot. This way you won't have to re-thread them for the next row. Instead of marking a guide line down the centre of the line of sewing, mark it next to where the edge of the foot will be. This makes it much easier to see.

Circular Sewing

This technique is used in the Dresden Plate block and the nine-patch cushion project. For circular sewing you will need a drawing pin with a flat top, a length of adhesive electrical tape about 4in (10cm) long, ¼in (6mm) masking tape, a pencil and a ruler.

1 Stick a strip of masking tape the radius of your finished circle to the right of your machine needle, going horizontally across the bed of your machine. Line up the top edge of the tape with the point of the needle (Fig 1). Some machines have a line going across which is in direct line with the needle. Using a pencil and ruler, draw a mark along the top edge of the tape. The distance from the needle to the mark should be the required radius of your first circle of stitching. From then on mark every ⅜in (1cm). This distance will produce circles that are quite close together. Making them ½in (1.3cm) apart would produce circles a little further apart and will enable those with wider (7mm or 9mm) stitches to use them. You could mark the first few at ⅜in (1cm) apart then continue with marks ½in (1.3cm) apart. This way you can sew smaller patterns at the centre and larger ones further out.

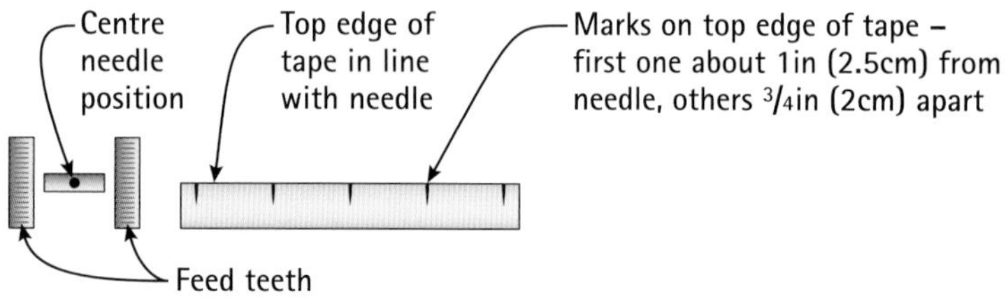

Figure 1 diagram labels:
- Centre needle position
- Top edge of tape in line with needle
- Marks on top edge of tape – first one about 1in (2.5cm) from needle, others ³⁄₄in (2cm) apart
- Feed teeth

Fig 1

2 Now cut two 2in (5cm) lengths of adhesive electrical tape and place the drawing pin, point side up on your sewing machine on the top of the masking tape at the first mark (Fig 2). If you use wider masking tape, the electrical tape will not be as secure. Stick one piece of electrical tape horizontally across the pin and the other piece vertically across the pin to secure it. Be careful not to stick the tape on the feed dogs. Check that the point of the drawing pin is in line with the needle, otherwise you will be sewing ovals instead of circles!

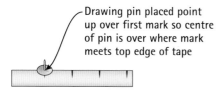

Figure 2 label: Drawing pin placed point up over first mark so centre of pin is over where mark meets top edge of tape

Fig 2

3 Find the centre of your piece of fabric and with a stabilizer underneath, push the centre over the drawing pin (see picture below). Select a decorative stitch and begin to sew. I suggest you sew on a practice piece first to see how the stitch pattern meets at the end. Allow the fabric to move by itself, you need only to guide it and make sure that the centre stays on the pin – it will go around in a circle. Press the 'Stop' or 'Pattern End' button when you reach the last stitch. Try not to use stitches that have a long backward motion as this tends to distort the circle. It does get easier as the circle gets larger. The shorter the stitches, the easier it is to meet up at the end of the circle. If you are a few stitches away from the end and it doesn't look as though it will meet up, try lengthening or shortening the stitch.

4 Remove the fabric from the pin. Lift the pin off the machine and stick it down again at the next mark to the right. Replace the centre of your fabric on the pin, select another stitch and sew as before. Repeat this procedure until you have the required diameter of stitching. If the hole in the fabric is getting a little large, iron on two small squares of fusible stabilizer, one on top of each other, on the back of the fabric over the hole.

Sewing Two Curved Sides that Meet at a Point

This technique is used in the Cutwork block and the covered box and varies slightly, depending on the needle's starting position.

Needle Starting at Centre Position

1 The technique is relatively easy if your decorative stitch begins with the needle in the centre position. Begin at the point with the needle and centre of the foot on the line and sew along the right-hand side of the curve, finishing at the end of a complete stitch pattern (Fig 1).

2 Begin at the point again, mirror imaging the design side to side if necessary, and sew along the left side of the curve (Fig 2).

Fig 1   Fig 2

Needle Starting to the Left

1 Scallops and some decorative stitches begin with the needle on the left. If you start with the needle on the line, the stitch will be sewn on the outside of the line, making your shape much wider than required and very difficult to keep in position (Fig 3). To overcome this, draw a line from the point down the centre of the oval. Start sewing at the point with the needle on the centre line and the centre of the foot on the curve (Fig 4).

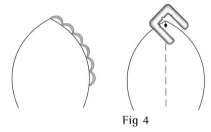

Fig 3   Fig 4

2 As you sew along the curve, keep the centre of the foot on the line, gradually turning the fabric and letting the needle go from side to side (Fig 5). To go down the other side, make sure you will be starting at the beginning of the stitch pattern by selecting the stitch again adjusted to the same settings, or by pressing the re-start button if you have one and then mirror image side to side. If you do not have a mirror image function then begin at the bottom of the shape in line with the end of the last pattern on the first side and sew towards the top point (see Mirror Imaging page 127). Alternatively, select a symmetrical stitch pattern. Place the needle in exactly the same place as the beginning of the first stitch on the right-hand side. There should be a thread tail on the top of your fabric to use as a guide. Position the centre of the foot on the curved line and sew down the left side (Fig 6).

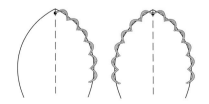

Fig 5   Fig 6

Couching

This technique is used in the Trapunto Corner block, the trapunto cushion project, the Shadow Appliqué block and in the borders. Couching is a method of sewing decorative braids and cords to a background fabric. A simple zigzag stitch is the most common one to use but any decorative stitch with a side to side action, such as a feather or cross stitch, would work well depending on the desired effect. There are some points to bear in mind when couching, as follows.

Couching Basics

- Decide on the look you want to achieve. For a more decorative effect, use an embroidery thread in the needle that contrasts with the background fabric and the cord and any side to side decorative stitch you like. To make the cord look as though it is woven into the background fabric, use the same colour thread in the needle as the background and a zigzag or ladder stitch. To make the cord to look as though it is floating on the fabric surface, use a needle thread to match the cord or a monofilament thread in the needle and a zigzag stitch.

- Use a presser foot that has a groove underneath about the same width as the cord you are couching. Most machines have a cording or braiding foot that either feeds the cord directly under the foot or through a hole or slot in the top of the foot. If you are unable to find a special cording/braiding foot, an embroidery foot, which has a groove underneath, will suffice. A braiding guide is very useful as it supports and feeds the cord without you having to hold it, leaving your hands free to guide the fabric.

- Draw the design line on the background fabric. Select a zigzag stitch (or other of your choice) and adjust the width so it just covers the cord. Leave a tail of cord at the beginning and secure the stitch. Sew over the cord, turning the fabric as needed to keep the drawn line under the centre of the foot. Secure the stitch at the end of your line and cut the cord, leaving a short tail. Use a needle with a large eye to pull the cord tails to the back.

- If there is a point in your design, stop with the needle down on the inside of the line (fig 1A). Pivot so the point in the design is at the side of the needle and adjust the stitch length to 0.0. Sew two stitches to secure the cord at the point, stopping on the inside of the line again (fig 1B). Pivot, lining up the fabric in the direction you will be sewing. Reset the stitch length to its original setting and continue (fig 1C).

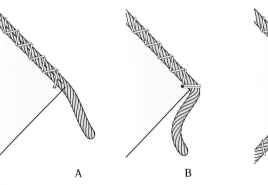

A   B   C

Fig 1

Wing Needle Sewing

This technique is used in the Dresden Plate block and the nine-patch cushion project. Wing needle sewing is one of my favourite techniques: I remember using a wing needle for the first time and thought it was magic! How such a simple thing like a needle and the same colour thread as the fabric can alter the look of a stitch is amazing.

In essence, a wing needle has a broad shaft that makes prominent holes in the fabric. These holes are the main focus of the stitch pattern, therefore a thread that matches the colour of the fabric should be used.

- Natural fabrics such as cotton, linen and silk give the best results. If your fabric is limp, then spray starch it before sewing as fabrics with more body are easier to work with. Always use a tear-away stabilizer and an embroidery or open-toe foot.

- Look at the stitches you have on your machine and choose the ones that go back and forth in the same place more than once. This will reinforce the holes made by the wing needle. Some of these may be labelled as stretch stitches on your machine, such as a zigzag that goes back and forth. Satin stitches and intricate patterns do not work well.

- If you don't have similar stitches to the ones shown in Fig 1 below then you could try those in Fig 2. These are sewn in adjoining rows and even a simple zigzag stitch would work well. To sew these, first sew a row of your chosen stitch, leave the needle in the fabric on the right. Turn the fabric clockwise 180° and then sew slowly down the other side, making sure the needle goes back in the holes down the centre. Use an open-toe foot so you can see the holes better.

- When sewing with a wing needle don't hold the fabric back, just guide it gently so that the needle pierces the same hole when it moves backwards.

Fig 1 Suggested stitches for wing needle sewing

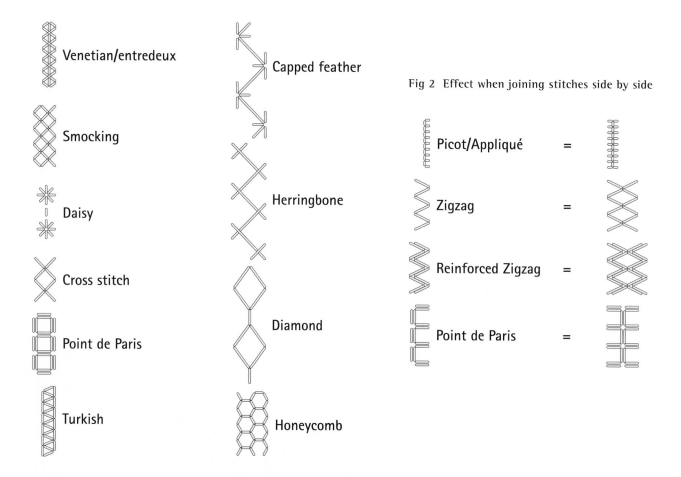

Candlewicking by Machine

This technique is used in the Dresden Plate block, nine-patch cushion, Cutwork block and the quilt borders. Some machines have a French knot or candlewicking stitch built in. If this is not available on your machine you may be able to programme the pattern in. There are two basic methods for doing this. The standard one is by using a zigzag stitch so the knot is formed sideways; the second method is to use the eight-directional feed menu found on some machines, so the stitch will sew a double stitch forwards and backwards – see Fig 1.

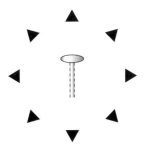

Fig 1

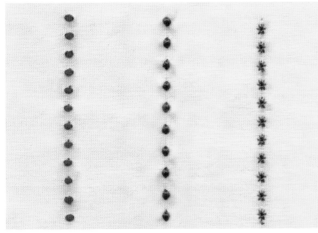

Side-to-side zigzag

Forward and back 8-directional feed

No programme a star with a reduced length and width

Method 1 programme (zigzag)

Programme = {zigzag: length 0.0, width 2.0} eight times
straight stitch: length 5.0.
If the needle pierces twice at one side of the zigzag stitches, solve the problem by mirror imaging every other zigzag when programming.

To prevent the needle hitting the centre of the knot before it sews the straight stitch, enter an additional zigzag (length 0.5, width 2.0), in the programme before the straight stitch.

Method 2 programme (eight-directional feed)

Programme = {double forward stitch, double backward stitch} five times
double forward
stitch straight stitch, length 5.0
The top tension may have to be loosened slightly (lower number). Use tear-away stabilizer under your fabric and a foot with a deep groove in the centre of the underside to allow the knots to feed through evenly. For sewing a candlewicking stitch that follows a curve, use a foot with a wider groove underneath. This gives more room for the knots to feed through that are slightly to one side because of the curve. There may be a special candlewicking foot for your machine, if not use an open-toe foot, beading foot, braiding foot or any foot with a groove in the centre.

I like to snip the straight stitches between the knots after all the candlewicking has been sewn. If you are concerned about the knot unravelling then enter a 'fix', if possible on your machine, before and after the zigzags or forward and reverse stitches. Be warned though, 'fixing' will make it extremely difficult to unpick should the need arise!

If you don't have a programming function, you may be able to select either a star, daisy, satin circle or any symmetrical stitch that repeats with a straight stitch between. Reduce the width and length so the stitch is quite tiny. If you are able to programme but unable to enter a zigzag with 0 length, then programme a star, daisy, satin circle or similar adjusted to a small length and width and then programme a long straight stitch. If you can't programme the long straight stitch (some machines enter up to five stitches at a time) then you may be able to programme a space stitch (a long straight stitch) which is usually found in the alphabet menu (_ or □).

Pulled Thread Sewing

This technique is used in the Dresden Plate block. For the best results in pulled thread work use a linen or loosely woven natural fabric. However, you could experiment with different fabrics, such as furnishing fabrics, metallic fabrics or silk. A shot silk can be very effective as the fibres are different shades. A fabric in a contrasting colour placed behind the pulled threads would be a stunning feature. Practise on a spare piece of fabric before you cut out your main pieces to decide whether you pull the threads on the straight or the crosswise grain. The basic steps are as follows.

1 Cut a strip of fabric so that the pulled threads will be parallel to the preferred grain. In the centre of the strip carefully pull out a section of threads in one direction of the fabric about ¼in (6mm) wide.

2 Using a wing needle and a thread to match your fabric, sew a triple straight stitch, sometimes referred to as a straight stretch stitch, down the centre of the line of pulled threads, trying to keep the gaps between the stitches even. If you don't have a triple stitch on your machine, then select a straight stitch. To help the threads to stay in bunches, stop with the needle down each time the stitch has moved backwards and with a pair of tweezers or quick unpick, open out the hole in front of the needle. Continue to the next reverse stitch and repeat the process. You may need to tighten the tension (a higher number) if the bunches of threads aren't tight enough.

3 When you have sewn down the centre, remove more threads either side of the stitching until the gap measures about ⅜in (1cm) or your required width.

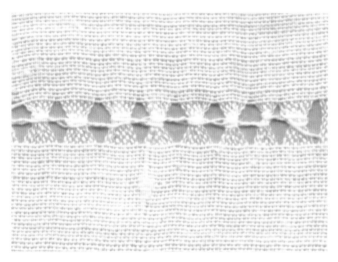

The pulled thread technique is easy but impressive, especially if a contrasting colour is placed underneath, which emphasizes the lacy effect.

The motifs in the centre of the Shadow Appliqué block (shown here) and the Cutwork block (opposite) use finished–edge appliqué.

Finished-Edge Appliqué

Using this method of appliqué gives you a wider choice of appliqué stitches because you don't have to be concerned about covering a raw edge. I most often use a buttonhole appliqué stitch. The settings are quite small (length 2.0, width 2.0). If you don't have this specific stitch on your machine you may have a stretch stitch or an overcasting stitch that looks similar. However, you may not be able to adjust this. A blind hem stitch will work, if adjusted to a narrow width and short length. So will a feather stitch or some of the other quilting stitches and even a small zigzag might work. Experiment! There are a few methods you can use to finish the edge. I used the following method in the Heirloom Quilt as it works well on silk.

1 Using iron-on interfacing, draw round the template on to the smooth (non-sticky) side. On your test pieces, try the same technique using the interfacing the other way up so that the sticky side will be on the inside when you have turned the shape through. This means you can iron it before applying it to the background fabric, giving it a firmer shape. However, you won't be able to stick it to the background as before and you are more likely to see a ridge on the front where the raw edge is. Decide which method you prefer. Instead of using interfacing, you could use a piece of the same fabric as the top of the design. This won't stick to the top or the background but the edge will be the same fabric on the front and back.

2 Do not add seam allowances and do not cut out yet. Place the interfacing, drawn side up, on to the right side of your appliqué fabric. Pin and machine on the line with a small straight stitch, sewing all the way around. If your fabric is very fine or 'floppy' (such as satin), place tear-away stabilizer underneath the fabric before sewing and remove it after sewing. Trim the surplus interfacing and fabric from the outside of the stitching line leaving about ¼in (6mm) seam allowance. Clip corners and curves. Make a slit in the middle of the interfacing about 1in (2.5cm) long and turn the appliqué shape right side out. Use a point turner to push the points out and go all the way around the seam line from the inside of the shape. Do not iron yet otherwise the interfacing will stick to the iron or the board!

3 Pin the shape in place on your background fabric. Iron in place carefully, as the interfacing will stick to the background. Sew around the edge with a buttonhole appliqué stitch or one of your choice. If your machine doesn't have this stitch you could use a small zigzag stitch or blind hem stitch adjusted shorter and narrower than the default setting – see Fig 1 for examples.

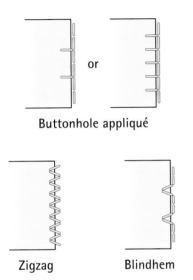

Buttonhole appliqué

Zigzag   **Blindhem**

Fig 1

To sew the buttonhole stitch, make sure that the horizontal stitches are pointing *towards* the appliqué shape and that the straight stitch sews right next to the shape into the background fabric (Fig 2). If the horizontal stitch is going to sew at a point, then stop with the needle in the fabric just before it is about to sew that stitch and turn the fabric so that the horizontal stitch sews in the centre of the point (Fig 3). Sew the stitch, stop with the needle in the fabric again and then turn the fabric in line with the next edge and continue sewing.

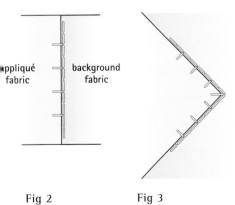

appliqué   background
fabric   fabric

Fig 2   **Fig 3**

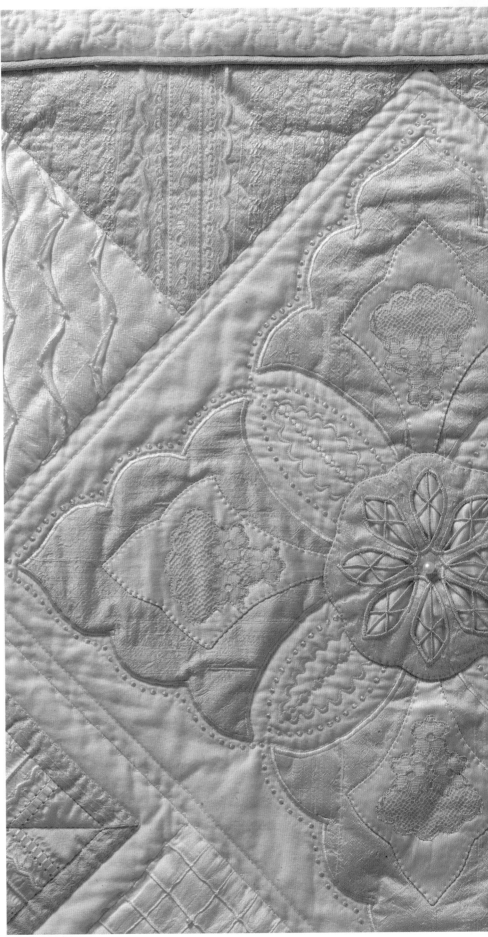

Satin Stitch Appliqué

This technique is used in the Dresden Plate block, the Cutwork block and the Shadow Appliqué block. Satin stitch is the usual stitch used to cover the raw edges of an appliqué shape. It is important that you sew the best satin stitch possible on your machine. There are a few basic techniques you can use to achieve this.

- Always use a tear-away stabilizer under your fabric.
- Spray starching the fabric will give even more stability but check on a scrap piece first as it can leave spots that are difficult to remove.
- A rayon thread in the top of the machine will give a slight sheen to the stitch which looks lovely against silk. A rayon of either 40 or 30 weight (which is slightly thicker) is best but test them both first. Try bobbin thread or standard 50 weight cotton or polyester machine sewing thread in the bobbin. It is important to try all these different variations as each one will produce a different tension.
- Use a Universal 70/10 or Embroidery 75/11 needle and an open-toe foot for satin-stitch appliqué.

Satin Stitch Settings

Some machines have a satin stitch as one of the stitch selections but for other machines you will have to adjust a zigzag stitch. Usually the two stitches are slightly different in the way they are formed. The built-in satin stitch will go straight across on every first stitch and then slant on every second stitch, whereas the zigzag will slant on every stitch – see Fig 1. Either way, begin with the width at 3.0 and the length at 0.3. (Refer also to important note about stitch length on page 104.)

The length (or density) of the stitch determines how close the stitches are. For the best look, the length needs to be quite close but not so close that it builds up on itself and gets caught in the machine. Look at the sides of the stitch – if you see any of the bobbin thread on the top you need to lower the top tension (a smaller number). Ideally you should see some of the top thread pulling through to the back. For those who have a built-in satin stitch you will notice that the tension has been automatically adjusted to a lower number.

Look at the sides of the stitches again to check that they are not making holes so close that it could weaken the fabric. If so, change to a smaller needle. If the stitch looks jagged at the sides change your needle to an Embroidery one or Sharp. This is due both to the weave of the fabric and the way the needle pierces it.

Having determined the best settings for a satin stitch, draw a line on scrap fabric and practise lining the stitch up at the edge, pretending that the appliqué is to the left of the line. About three-quarters of the stitch should be over the appliqué on the left of the line and the other quarter on the background to the right of the line – see Fig 2.

Sewing Curves

On gradual curves, it's best to guide the fabric smoothly round without pivoting. However, on sharper curves you will need to stop and pivot the fabric. Pivoting on the wrong side of a curve will result in gaps on the edge – see Fig 3. The needle should be left in the fabric while turning or pivoting. It is important to keep the shape of the curve and stitch without any jagged edges. Assuming the appliqué fabric is to the left of the needle, the golden rule is:

On inside curves stop with the needle on the left;

On outside curves stop with the needle on the right.

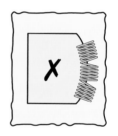 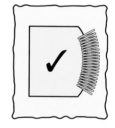

Fig 3a outside curves

 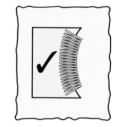

Fig 3b inside curves

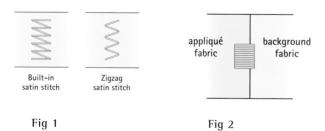

Built-in satin stitch	Zigzag satin stitch

Fig 1

appliqué fabric | background fabric

Fig 2

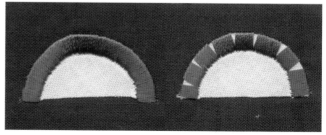

Correct satin stitch   Incorrect

Sewing Corners

There are a several methods you can use to sew corners and the one most often used is Method 1, described below. However, because there are two layers of stitches on top of each other right on the corner, this can show clumps of stitching, resulting in the fabric getting caught under the foot. Method 2 looks good on paper but is very difficult to sew, and not all machines have the function to taper the stitch at both sides individually and the stitches at the point of the corner are very tiny indeed. I always use Method 3 because it looks good and, once mastered, is easy to use.

Method 1

Sew a few stitches beyond the corner and stop with the needle on the outside (in the background). Lift the presser foot, pivot the fabric and sew over the previous stitches at the corner. Continue sewing down the next side (Fig 4).

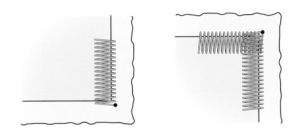

Fig 4

Method 2

On some makes of machines you are able to mitre a corner. To do this you will need to be able to adjust the stitch width from the left and the right side independently. Some machines only adjust the width from both sides at the same time, which will not work for this type of corner. Sew a few stitches beyond the corner, leaving the needle on the outside. Lift the presser foot and pivot the fabric. Bring the needle out of the fabric, adjust the stitch width to 0.5mm and lower the needle into the same hole it came out of. Lower the presser foot and, as you are stitching, gradually increase the stitch width so that at the bottom of the corner the stitch is the same width as the stitching on the previous side (Fig 5).

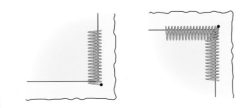

Fig 5

Method 3 (preferred)

Sew a few stitches beyond the corner and stop with the needle in the fabric on the left (appliqué side). Keeping the needle in the fabric, lift the presser foot and pivot the fabric 90° so the next edge to be sewn is in front of the needle. With the presser foot still up, turn the hand wheel towards you until the needle comes out of the fabric and swings to the right. Move the fabric slightly and turn the hand wheel until the needle goes back down into the same hole it came out of. Lower the presser foot and continue sewing (Fig 6).

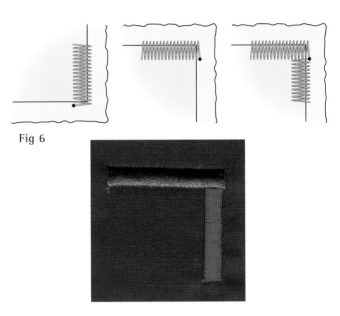

Fig 6

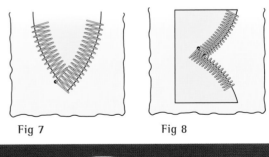

Sewing Points

When sewing outside points, as you approach the point, guide your fabric so that the stitches are sewing at the same angle as the next edge you will be satin stitching (Fig 7).

When sewing inside points or corners, stop with the needle in the fabric on the left (in the appliqué fabric) just before the point. Pivot and bring needle out of fabric and then back in at the same place and continue along the other edge (Fig 8).

Fig 7   **Fig 8**

Sewing inside and outside points

Shadow Appliqué

This technique is used in the Shadow Appliqué block. You will need to use a double-sided fusible web for shadow appliqué work. There are different makes on the market. The easiest to find is Bondaweb (Wonder Under) which will suffice, but if you can find it, I much prefer Steam-A-Seam 2. This product sticks to the fabric for a temporary hold and can then be re-positioned. Once ironed, it will fuse and give a permanent bond. You will also need a sheer fabric to cover the shapes, such as organza (silk or polyester) or net. The fabrics used for the appliqué shapes should be deeper shades than the required finished shades as the sheer fabric will mute the colours a little.

1 If you are using Bondaweb, place the appliqué shapes with the front of the shape facing the smooth side of the Bondaweb and draw around the outside of the shapes. If you are using Steam-A-Seam 2, peel it apart a little at the corner to determine which side to draw on. On the paper that has the web still attached to it, place the front of the appliqué shapes facing the paper and draw around the outside of the shapes. Cut around the shapes leaving a small allowance around the edge. For Bondaweb, iron the shapes to the wrong side of your appliqué fabric. For Steam-A-Seam 2, peel off the backing paper and stick the shapes to the wrong side of the appliqué fabric. Cut the fusible web and the material together on the drawn line. Peel off the backing paper and iron the appliqué shapes to the background fabric.

2 When all the appliqué shapes are in position, cover with a piece of sheer fabric and pin or tack (baste) securely all round.

3 Using a straight stitch (length 2.0) open-toe foot and needle down position, very slowly machine around the edge of the shapes – the smaller the shapes, the trickier it is! You almost have to sew one stitch at a time to make sure that you keep exactly on the edge of the appliqué fabric underneath the sheer top (Fig 1). Do not secure the stitches at either end as this will leave an unsightly blob – you will need to leave thread ends, pull them through to the back and tie them off instead. It is a little time consuming but well worth it for the effect.

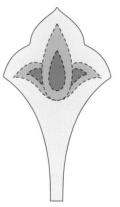

Fig 1

Lace Shaping

This technique is used in the Shadow Appliqué block. To shape lace, you will need to use special cotton lace that has a 'header', which is a thread running through the straight edge of the lace that can be pulled up to for shaping the lace around curves. If you have difficulty finding this, you can machine a straight stitch (length 3.0) along the top edge of a length of edging lace, leaving thread tails for pulling up. You will also need pins without plastic heads, spray starch and a lace shaping board (or any padded surface like an ironing board).

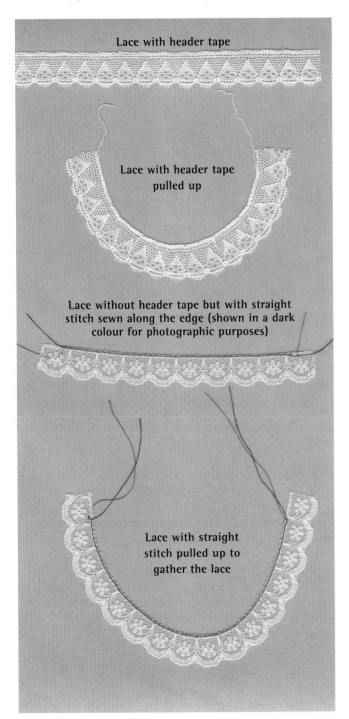

Lace with header tape

Lace with header tape pulled up

Lace without header tape but with straight stitch sewn along the edge (shown in a dark colour for photographic purposes)

Lace with straight stitch pulled up to gather the lace

1 Make a template of your finished shape. Draw round the template either on to your fabric or on to a scrap piece of fabric. Draw a bisecting line through each angle where the lace will be mitred. These need to be about 5cm (2in) long from the angle towards the inside of the shape (see Fig 1).

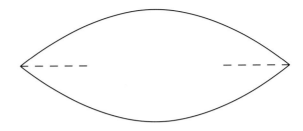

Fig 1

2 Place the fabric with the drawn shape on a lace shaping board and iron your lace flat. Begin at the bottom of your shape at a mitre if there is one. Leave about a 1in (2.5cm) tail of lace and pin the outside edge of the lace (i.e., the edge without the header) on the line at point A in Fig 2. If you have a mitre, then place another pin on the inside edge of the lace along the bisecting line at point B. If there is no mitre, then place a pin opposite point A on the inside edge of the lace (Fig 3). The pins should go through the lace, the fabric and the board at an angle that is as flat as possible to the board, with the head pointing away from the edge of the lace. The header edge of the lace should be on the inner edge of the curve.

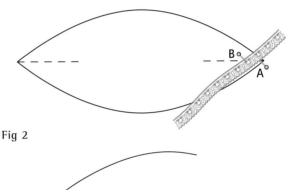

Fig 2

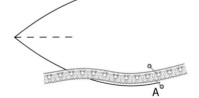

Fig 3

3 Guide the outside edge of the lace along the template line, placing pins every so often to secure it (see Fig 4) – the sharper the curves, the more pins are required.

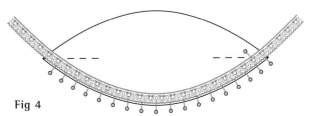

Fig 4

119

4 When you reach a bisecting line, place a pin at point C (the outer point of the mitre) and another at point D (the inner point of the mitre) along the bisecting line (Fig 5). Fold the lace back on top of itself. Remove the pin at point D and replace through both layers of lace and into the board. You should have a small pleat of lace at point D (Fig 6). Continue pinning the outside of the lace around the template shape. You will have a perfect mitre at point D (Fig 7). Repeat this process for each mitre.

6 To finish the ends of lace at a mitre, cross the end of your lace over the beginning tail at point B (Fig 9). Remove the pin at point B and replace it, going through both pieces of lace. Fold under the top piece of lace so that it lies on top of the beginning tail of lace and leave the pin in (Fig 10). Cut the ends off that are outside the edge of the top lace and replace the pin at point A, going through both pieces of lace (Fig 11).

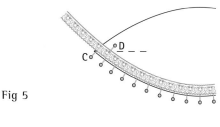

Fig 5

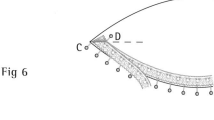

Fig 6

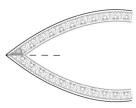

Fig 7

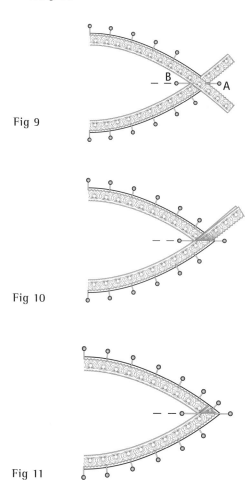

Fig 9

Fig 10

Fig 11

5 To remove the fullness at the inner edge of the lace along the curves, simply pull the header thread until the lace lies flat and pin it to the board (Fig 8). The header thread is usually the very top one and slightly thicker than the rest. If you have a loop of header thread that you pulled, pin this to the board, and sew it in when you attach the lace to your fabric.

7 Leaving the pins in place, spray starch the shaped lace and press. Remove the pins carefully. If you shaped your lace directly on to the background fabric, then pin the lace to the background. If you shaped your lace on to a scrap piece of fabric, carefully lift the lace off the board and pin it to the background fabric.

8 Sew the lace to your fabric using a small zigzag stitch, a straight stitch or machine entredeux stitch around the inside and outside edges. Place tear-away stabilizer underneath before you sew.

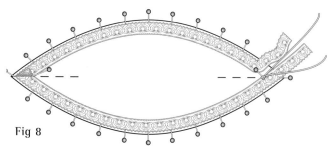

Fig 8

Sewing Lace Motifs

This technique is used in the Cutwork block of the Heirloom Quilt. When sewing lace motifs your motif could either be a finished-edge lace shape (purchased or sewn on your embroidery machine) or a shape within a larger piece of lace. A few of the ladies attending my Heirloom Quilt classes have used lace motifs cut from their wedding dress and some have even used antique lace found amongst their mother's treasures, which I think adds a very special touch to the quilt.

Bear the following points in mind when sewing lace motifs.

- If the motif you want to use is within a larger piece of lace, cut around the edge of the shape very carefully, trying not to snip the edge of the design. You could use an erasable marker to draw around the shape before you begin cutting.

- Place the shape on to your background fabric and pin it in place with the points of the pins facing the outside edge of the motif. Using a fabric glue stick before you pin helps to hold it in place. Because the motif has a sewn outline, you don't have to be concerned about it unravelling or fraying, so it only has to be sewn to the background with a stitch that barely shows. Either a straight stitch or zigzag stitch will work, depending on the design.

- Use a thread that matches the lace as closely as possible. If your motif was made using a shiny or rayon thread, then use a rayon embroidery thread to sew it on to your background. If, however, it has a dull finish, then use a cotton or polyester thread.

Machine Lace

This technique is used in the Lace and Twin Needle block. Machine lace is made by sewing decorative stitches on a very fine base such as bridal tulle or organza. Cotton tulle, which is quite expensive and not easy to find, is a little too thick. I prefer to use bridal tulle as this looks more authentic than organza, however, because it is a little stretchy and has holes, it can be more difficult to sew on. Practise on both bases to see which you prefer.

If you choose to use tulle, then you will notice that when the stabilizer is washed away, some stitches may look a little distorted. This is because parts of the stitch pattern are in a hole! This is more noticeable on satin stitches, especially the scallop ones. To overcome this, place a strip of organza under the scallop stitches at the edge before sewing. Cut the surplus organza away afterwards from the inside of the stitch. The organza on the outside of the stitch is cut away with the tulle.

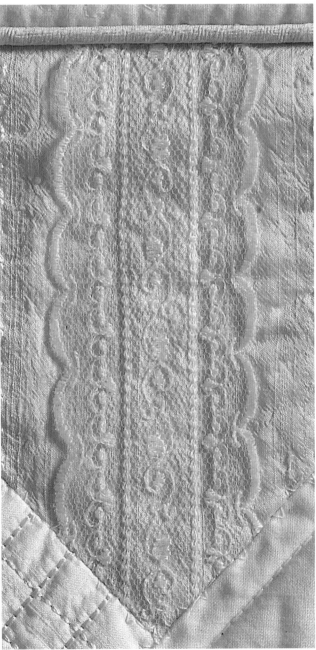

A few pretty lace motifs that would look good in the Heirloom Quilt.

Using Water-Soluble Stabilizers

There are a few different water-soluble stabilizers on the market. The most popular is a thin plastic such as Sulky Solvy or Floriana Water-Soluble Topping, which work well but may stick a little to the needle plate and bunch up. Another one is a woven fabric type such as Solvy Cold Water Soluble or Floriana Wet N Gone (which is the one I normally use). This works well, especially if you use two layers. Madeira also produce a water-soluble paper. All three types will work for sewing lace. Experiment with different ones to determine which works the best in your machine. For more stability, if needed, put the stabilizer and sheer fabric in a hoop before sewing.

1 Use a 40 weight embroidery thread in the top and bobbin thread in the bobbin. I used white on the Heirloom Quilt, but you could use a contrasting colour thread. A size 60 needle should be used for organza, but a 70 will be fine for tulle.

2 Cut a strip of base fabric 1in (2.5cm) wider and longer than required and place a strip of water-soluble stabilizer the same size underneath. A water-soluble stabilizer is used so that none of it remains after soaking, whereas a regular tear-away stabilizer will show through the sheer base. I prefer to use two layers of water-soluble fabric, such as Floriana Wet N Gone.

3 Draw a line down the centre of the base fabric and a line about ¼in (6mm) from the top with a water-soluble marker – it will be washed away with the stabilizer.

4 Select a stitch pattern that is not too heavily satin stitched but one that will show up. Begin on the line at the top and sew down the centre line. At the end of the row secure the stitch and cut the threads. Select another stitch pattern. Begin at the top line, guiding the foot next to the centre row of stitches. Sew to the end, fix, cut and clip the thread end. Restart the stitch pattern and mirror image if needed to sew down the other side of the centre.

5 Continue in this way until you have the required width of stitches. A scallop stitch on the edges looks effective. If you choose to do this and are using tulle as your base, place a strip of organza underneath to prevent stitch distortion, which can happen because of the holes in the tulle.

6 Carefully wash away the stabilizer and pat dry with a towel. Trim the net and/or organza away from the outside edges close to the stitches. If you used a strip of organza under the scallop stitches, then trim this away as well. Press the finished lace with a *warm* iron (not hot, otherwise it will shrivel up!) or allow it to dry naturally. Make sure that the entire stabilizer is washed away, otherwise the lace will stick to the ironing board!

Cutwork

This technique is used in the Cutwork block with Richelieu bars and without bars in the covered box project. When machining a cutwork design, it is better to place the fabric in a hoop, although it can be done without. There are slight variations in the method used, but I have found the following one to be the best.

1 Draw your design on a square of tear-away stabilizer, larger than your hoop size. Place the fabric wrong side up, place a square of water-soluble stabilizer (such as Solvy) on top, and then place the tear-away stabilizer on top of that with the drawn side up. Secure the three fabrics in an embroidery hoop, placing the inner hoop on top first and the outer hoop underneath. Tighten the hoop so the fabrics are taut.

2 Thread your machine with 50 weight polyester on top and in the bobbin in a shade to match your fabric. Slide the hoop under the machine needle with the drawn side up and sew around the design with a small zigzag stitch, keeping the line under the centre of the foot (Fig 1). Don't sew the lines for the Richelieu bars, only the cutwork shapes.

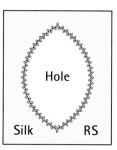

Fig 1

3 Using small, sharp scissors, cut the fabric and the tear-away stabilizer from inside all of the cutwork areas, leaving the water-soluble stabilizer in place. Try to trim as close to the stitching as possible. Do not worry if you cut parts of the water-soluble stabilizer as there will be another piece put underneath.

4 Remove the fabrics from the hoop and place another square of thin water-soluble stabilizer underneath the tear-away stabilizer. Secure in the hoop again with the right side of the silk uppermost and the second square of water-soluble stabilizer underneath.

5 If you are making Richelieu bars, these need to be sewn at this point. Thread your machine with rayon 40 weight on the top and in the bobbin and mark the lines of the bars on the water-soluble stabilizer. Using a straight stitch, length 2.5, secure the stitch in the fabric at the beginning of the bar. Sew straight across on the stabilizer to the opposite edge (Fig 2.) Leave the needle in the fabric, pivot and sew back across the same line.

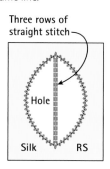

Fig 2

6 Sew one more line (three lines in total) and then pivot again and sew over the three lines with a small zigzag stitch (length 0.5, width 1.0), making sure you encase the straight lines in the zigzag (Fig 3). Sew around the edge using a zigzag or straight stitch to the next bar point and proceed as before (Fig 4).

7 When all bars have been sewn, sew a satin stitch, width 2.5, around the edges of the holes. One swing of the needle should be piercing the stabilizer right next to the cut edge, while the other swing of the needle should be going into the fabric, completely covering the first zigzag stitching (Fig 5). Most of the water-soluble stabilizer can then be carefully ripped away. Any remaining stabilizer will disappear by dabbing with a wet cotton bud or swab (Q-tip).

Zigzag stitch over the straight stitches

Fig 3

Fig 4

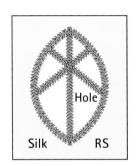

Fig 5

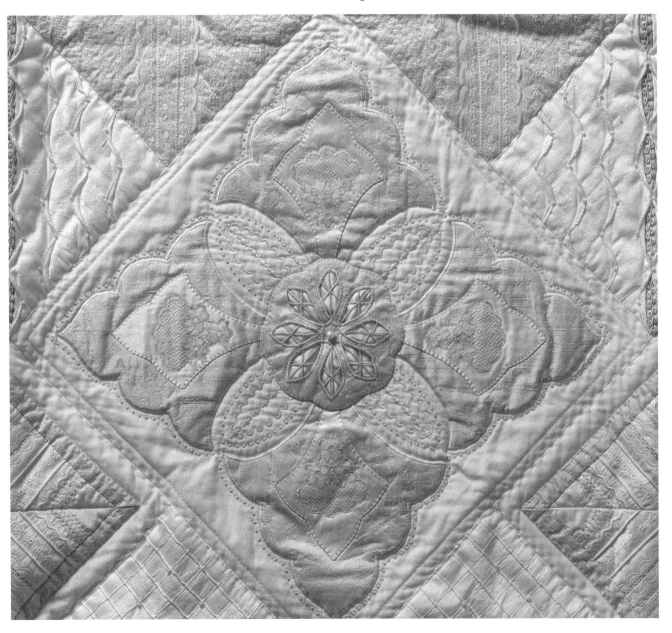

Puffing

This technique is used in the Puffing block (shown below) and the roll pillow project. Puffing is the name for a strip of fabric gathered along each long edge. This results in an insertion that can be used straight or curved and even embellished to add texture to any decorative project. Most makes of machine have a gathering foot as an additional accessory. The foot usually has two flat plates with a slot between them, as shown right.

You will need to start by cutting a narrow strip of woven light fabric approximately 2in (5cm) wide x three times the required finished length. The length of the strip should run parallel to the straight grain if you are using silk, but perpendicular to the straight grain if not, although you should test both grains first to determine which gives a better result.

For Machines with a Gathering Foot Attachment

1 Attach the gathering foot and select a straight stitch, length 4. Use regular machine sewing thread in the top and bobbin. Place the fabric underneath both of the flat plates of the foot. (The slot is used to place another fabric in whilst gathering the one underneath. The fabric in the slot is not gathered but is sewn to the gathered strip.) Sew slowly at an even speed, lining up the right edge of the foot with the edge of the fabric. For tighter gathers, increase the upper tension and/or lengthen the stitch.

2 Flip the fabric strip over and sew down the other edge. When you have gathered both edges, hold opposite edges and, moving down the strip a few inches at a time, pull out to even the gathers (Fig 1).

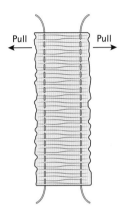

Fig 1

For Machines without a Gathering Foot

If your machine doesn't have a gathering foot there are two methods you can use for puffing.

Method 1

1 Using the standard presser foot, set your machine to a straight stitch, length 4.0, and lower the top tension. Leave thread tails at the beginning and end and do not secure the stitches. Sew slowly at an even speed, lining up the right edge of the foot with the edge of the fabric. Sew to the end of the strip and remove the strip from the machine leaving long thread tails. Do not secure the stitches.

2 Sew another row using the same settings, lining up the right edge of the foot with the previous line of stitching (Fig 2). Flip the fabric over and repeat along the other long edge.

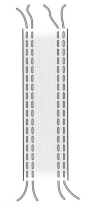

Fig 2

3 Pull the bobbin thread tails to gather the two edges and adjust the gathers so they are even and the strip is the required length (Fig 3).

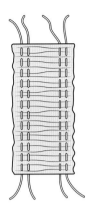

Fig 3

4 You will have two rows of stitching along both long edges. When the strips are inserted into your work you will sew between the two rows of gathering stitches at either side. This will not only make it easier to remove the gathering threads, but give a more even gather.

Method 2

1 Using the embroidery foot, set your machine to zigzag, length 3.0, width 3.0. Cut a length of narrow cord (similar to crochet cord) a little longer than the length of your strip.

2 Place the cord under the middle of the foot, and the outside edge of the foot on the edge of the fabric. Sew down the right edge of the fabric making sure that the zigzag stitch sews *over* the cord and not through it. Turn the strip around and repeat for the other edge of the fabric strip (Fig 4).

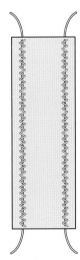

Fig 4

3 Pull the cords up on both sides to gather the strip, making them even and the strip the required finished length.

4 When inserting your strip, sew just to the inside of the zigzag, which will allow you to remove the cord easily.

Faggoting

This technique is used in the Puffing block and the roll pillow project. Faggoting is the term used for joining two folded edges with a decorative stitch. There is often a gap left between the two edges. There are different methods of achieving this depending on your machine and its accessories. You could use a hemstitching foot or a tailor tacking or marking foot, but I think the method below works best.

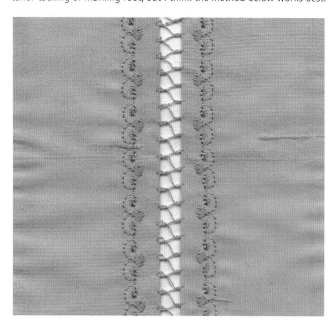

1 Fold under the edges of the two pieces of fabric approximately ½in (1.3cm) to the wrong side. Spray starch and/or use a strip of tear-away stabilizer under each edge making sure the stabilizer doesn't show beyond the folded edges.

2 Use the same thread on the top and in the bobbin. A contrasting colour to the fabric will make the stitches show up better. The most effective stitch to use is a feather stitch (Fig 1) but if you don't have this stitch on your machine, the stitch patterns shown in Fig 2 can be used. Practise first and adjust the stitch to its widest setting.

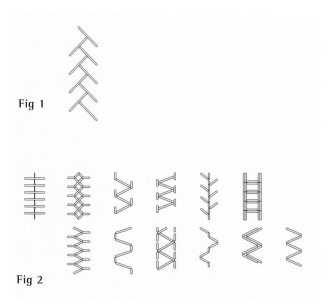

Fig 1

Fig 2

3 As the two edges are fed into the machine, there needs to be a gap of approximately ¼in (6mm) between them, slightly less than the width of your chosen stitch. The stitch should go into each folded edge and across the gap. If the fabric puckers then loosen the top tension a little (lower number).

Keeping the Gap Even

There are a few ways to keep the gap even in faggoting, as follows.
- The easiest is to use a faggoting or Spanish hemstitch foot. This foot will not only guide the edges evenly but has a groove for inserting a cord between the gap. Unfortunately this foot is not available for all machines.
- Some machines have markings on the stitch plate or a foot that can be used to guide the folded edges either side. You can also use a plastic coffee stirrer, or a narrow strip of template plastic, or a narrow bias bar taped in front of the needle.
- Another way to keep the gap even is to draw two parallel lines the width of the required gap apart on a strip of water-soluble paper. Machine tack (baste) the edges to be faggoted next to the drawn lines. After you've sewn your decorative stitch, remove the tacking (basting) stitches and carefully cut away as much of the stabilizer as possible. Rinse any remaining stabilizer from behind the stitching.

Securing the Seam Allowances

When you have sewn the faggoting, you will need to secure the fabric edges that are turned under on either side of the gap as they could pull inwards and thus not lie flat. Place a strip of organza or contrasting fabric under the faggoting at the same time to keep the gap open – see Fig 3 below. A few other ideas are as follows:
- Use a wing needle stitch, decorative stitch or scallop either side and then trim away the excess fabric on the underside. Make sure you use tear-away stabilizer underneath.
- Fold a tuck either side to hide the raw edges.
- Sew a seam either side, trapping the raw edges in the seam.

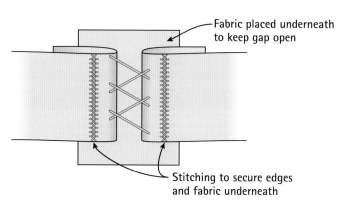

Fabric placed underneath to keep gap open

Stitching to secure edges and fabric underneath

Fig 3

Mirror Imaging

This technique is used in the Puffing block and the roll pillow project. The technique applies if you want to sew two rows of decorative stitching opposite each other, with one row of stitches facing the opposite way. If you don't have a mirror image function on your machine see the method opposite.

Using a Machine with a Mirror Image Function

1 For the stitch patterns to line up, draw a line at the top where both rows of stitching will start and adjust your chosen stitch pattern to the required length and width. Beginning at the line, sew the first row of stitches and press the 'Stop' or 'Pattern End' button if you have one to stop the row at the end of a complete stitch pattern (Fig 1). Remove the Stop/Pattern End function.

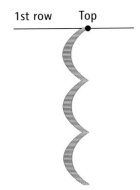

Fig 1

2 Mirror image your stitch pattern side to side and beginning at the line, sew down the other side (Fig 2). Before sewing the second side, draw a line at the end of about every second or third stitch pattern on the first row. When you sew the second row, keep the Stop/ Pattern End button on and use these lines as a guide for where the stitch patterns should end. If the pattern finishes before the line, then pull the fabric through very slightly for the next pattern. Similarly, if it finishes beyond the line, hold the fabric back a little.

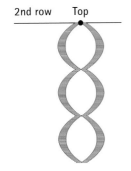

Fig 2

Faggoting is beautifully enhanced by mirror image stitching, as shown here with these satin stitch scallops.

3 Sometimes, however careful you are the stitch patterns don't line up exactly. To correct this, first make sure that you are using the correct presser foot and try adjusting the foot pressure to a higher number, as this will help to feed the fabric more evenly. It is also important to sew at the same even speed for both sides. Make sure you feed the fabric in straight, as if it is at a slight angle it will affect the length of the pattern.

Using a Machine without a Mirror Image Function

If you don't have a mirror image function on your machine, sew the first row as step 1 opposite, finishing at the end of a stitch pattern and marking a line across the bottom of the last stitch pattern (Fig 3). Turn your work the other way around and begin the second row on the line you just marked (Fig 4).

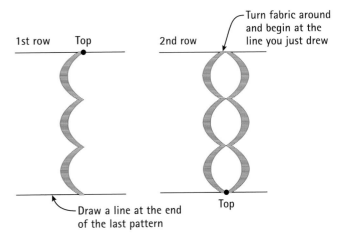

Fig 3   **Fig 4**

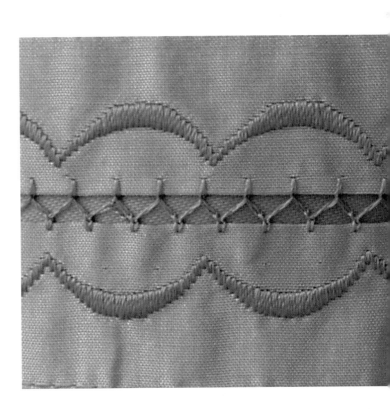

Corded Entredeux

This technique is used in the Puffing block. The entredeux stitch (see Fig 1 below) is sometimes referred to as Venetian hemstitch and is sewn using a wing needle (see Wing Needle Sewing on page 112). Sewing this stitch over cord makes it more defined. There are a few alternative stitches that work just as well with a wing needle and cord so experiment with the ones you have on your machine.

A fine cord (such as a perlé size 5, 8 or 12 or crochet cotton) that matches the colour of your thread and fabric looks best with the entredeux stitch (Fig 1).

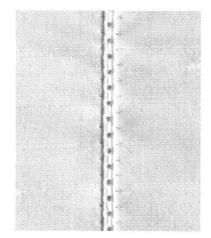

Fig 1

Use a foot that has at least two grooves underneath and/or holes in the top to thread the cords through. The two grooves either side of the centre groove on a pin-tucking foot, or the first two holes on a seven-hole cording foot, or the two grooves either side of the centre on a cording foot that has three grooves on the top should work. You may have a different foot that can be used for your machine. Some machines have a foot with two grooves underneath, used for sewing buttonholes (not the automatic type), which works well for this technique. The two grooves or holes need to be either side of the centre of the foot.

Cut two pieces of cord at least the length of your row of stitching. Place these in the grooves or holes of the presser foot, keeping them straight and parallel as you sew. Place tear-away stabilizer underneath and insert a wing needle. Adjust the stitch width so that both side swings of the stitch sew over the cords. Be careful when you sew the stitches that you sew over the cord *without piercing it*.

Decorative Twin Needle Sewing

This technique is used in the Lace and Twin Needle block. A twin needle can be fitted in most machines – you only need an extra thread spindle for a second top thread. As only one bobbin thread is used, it forms a zigzag stitch on the underside, producing a slight stretch in the stitch. Because of this stretch quality in the stitch you can use a 4mm or 6mm twin needle to turn up hems on stretch fabrics.

Sewing with Twin Needles

Twin needles come in different sizes. The first number on the packet refers to the distance in millimetres the two needles are apart, which ranges from 1.6 to 7.0. The second number refers to the thickness of the needle. Usually 1.6–3.5 will be an 80 and 4.0–7.0 will be 100. Stretch twin needles are also available in size 75. The best size to use for decorative stitches is 2.0mm. If a smaller needle is used, the stitches are too close together and don't give the required effect. Any wider and the width of the stitch pattern will have to be limited too much.

When sewing decorative stitches with a twin needle, care has to be taken not to allow the stitch to swing so wide that it hits the side of the foot and stitch plate. The wider the needles are apart, the more likely this is to happen. Most computer machines have a twin needle guard which, when selected, will limit the stitch width. However, not all machines will allow you to select the exact size of the needle you are using and will usually set it for a 3.0mm needle. This will not give you a wide enough stitch if you are using a 2.0mm twin needle and therefore is best not used. You must, however reduce the stitch width each time you select a stitch, to no more than 4.0 on a 6.0mm stitch plate, 5.0 on a 7.0mm stitch plate and 7.0 on a 9.0mm plate.

Thread your machine with two reels of 40 weight embroidery thread on the top. These can either be the same colour, two completely different colours or two different shades of the same colour, giving a shadow effect. Refer to your machine instructions for threading.

Use an open-toe or embroidery foot. A pin-tucking foot is not required as unlike the twin needle pin-tucks, you are not aiming to produce a raised effect – except, maybe, for the single line stitches. Use tear-away stabilizer beneath, remove it after each row of sewing, then replace it for the next row. Before you begin each new stitch pattern, double check that you have limited the stitch width. Some stitches work better than others. The picture below shows some effective ones but you will discover more on your machine. Try different ones on scrap fabric. You may need to lengthen the stitches, otherwise, with two needles, the sewing is likely to bunch up, especially if a satin type stitch is used.

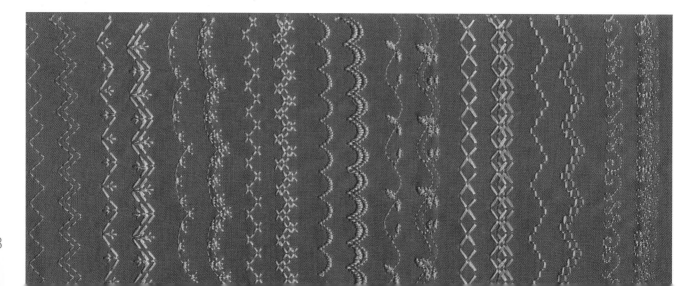

Twin Needle Pin-Tucks

This technique is used in the Puffing block and the roll pillow project. Twin needles come in various sizes – an example is shown here. For pin-tucks I use a 1.6mm, 2.0mm or 2.5mm twin needle. See also Decorative Twin Needle Sewing opposite and Crosshatching overleaf.

Use two 50 weight threads in the top. Try to keep them separate at the last thread guide, i.e., the guide just above the needle, by placing one thread either side or leaving one out of the guide, depending on your machine. Refer to your machine manual if you are unsure.

A pin-tucking foot helps to keep the tucks parallel and this type of foot is available in different sizes, ranging from three to nine grooves. The closer the needles are together, the more grooves you will need under the foot. Therefore, if you use a 1.6mm needle, it would be best to use a nine-groove pin-tucking foot. For a 3.0mm needle use a five-groove foot.

Getting Started

Insert a 2.0mm or 2.5mm twin needle and thread your machine with two threads in the top. Mark a line where your pin-tuck is to be sewn and attach a five- or seven-groove pin-tucking foot. Select a straight stitch, length 2.0, and lower the presser foot at the top of the line. Hold the thread tails and sew down the line.

If you want to sew more than one row of pin-tucks next to each other, sew the first row of pin-tucks (Fig 1) and then position the row under the groove in the foot to the right or left of the centre (Fig 2). This will keep your rows parallel. For the next row, line up the last pin-tuck in the same groove as before. If you want a wider distance between the pin-tucks, line the row just sewn under the second groove next to the centre one.

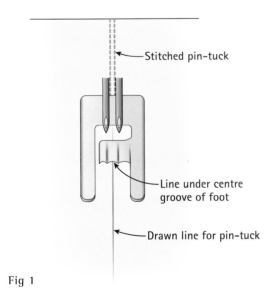

— Stitched pin-tuck

— Line under centre groove of foot

— Drawn line for pin-tuck

Fig 1

Second pin-tuck → ← First pin-tuck

← First pin-tuck fed under groove to right of centre groove (This keeps second pin-tuck parallel)

Fig 2

Creating a Raised Effect

A raised effect in pin-tucking is very attractive – here are a few things to try to produce such an effect.

- Cord the tucks by placing a fine cord such as crochet cotton or perlé thread underneath the fabric. Some machines have a hole in the stitch plate and others a separate grooved guide that is clipped to the stitch plate in front of the needle to guide the cord.
- Sew along the cross grain of the fabric, holding the fabric taut in front and behind the needle. This will not only raise the tuck but will help prevent any puckering.
- Tighten the bobbin tension a little by turning the screw about 90° clockwise (this is only recommended if you own a separate bobbin case otherwise it can be difficult to reset it to its original position).
- Iron a fold in the fabric where the pin-tuck is to be sewn and open it out before stitching. This is very effective as it creates a ridge before you sew.
- Shorten the stitch length.
- Try a narrower twin needle.
- Do not use a stabilizer.

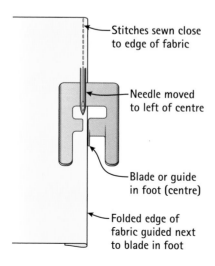

Crosshatching

This technique is used in the Crosshatched block of the Heirloom Quilt. Crosshatching is the term used for pin-tucks that are sewn in parallel rows in one direction, with another set of parallel rows sewn in the opposite direction forming a grid. The tucks may be sewn either with a twin needle or by edge stitching along the fold of the fabric, which is the method I prefer. You will need to choose a marking tool that is best for your fabric but not a water-soluble one as the marks will set when ironed and be difficult to remove. I find that a white chalk wheel works quite well on most fabrics. As you will be pressing a crease along each marked line, a hera marker would also be a good choice.

1 On the wrong side of your fabric, make small marks along the top and bottom edge your chosen distance apart. In the Crosshatched block mine were ¾in (1.9cm) apart, resulting in squares slightly smaller than ¾in (1.9cm) when finished.

2 Put the fabric wrong side up on a soft surface, such as an ironing board, and place a ruler just under the first mark on each edge. Take a hera marker and press it on the fabric along the edge of the ruler. Lift the ruler off, fold the fabric wrong sides together along the crease you have just made and press with an iron. Open the fabric out and repeat for the remaining marks.

3 Thread your machine with the same thread in the top and the bobbin, as both sides of the tucks will be visible and should look the same. Select a straight stitch, length 2.0–2.5. You will need to sew very closely to the folded edge so using a foot with a guide in the centre, such as an edge-joining or ditch quilting foot, will help tremendously. To use this, position the fabric under the machine with the fold right next to the left of the guide in the foot (Fig 1). Move the needle to the left approximately ⅛in (3mm). Sew very slowly, keeping the fold next to the guide. If you don't have a similar foot you may be able to use a blind hem foot but be careful about moving the needle in case it comes down on the bend in the guide causing the needle to break. If this foot doesn't work then use a regular stitching foot and guide the fabric very slowly. An open-toe foot would not work well as it doesn't give enough support to the edge.

Stitches sewn close to edge of fabric

Needle moved to left of centre

Blade or guide in foot (centre)

Folded edge of fabric guided next to blade in foot

Fig 1

4 When all the tucks in one direction have been sewn, iron them from the right side first to make sure they all lie in the same direction then iron on the back.

5 Now mark lines in the opposite direction, press a fold along each line and sew as before, being careful when you cross the first set of tucks at each junction.

Machine Quilting

Once the layers of quilt top, wadding (batting) and backing have been tacked (basted) and/or pinned in place, you are ready to begin quilting. Quilting not only keeps the layers together but adds that touchy-feely element to your quilt.

Machine Quilting Needle and Foot

A machine quilting needle is the best one to use as it is designed to pierce through all the layers. A walking foot, sometimes referred to as an even-feed or dual-feed foot is a must for sewing long, relatively straight lines. Without this foot, the fabric is only being fed through the machine by the machine's feed dogs. As the quilt is quite thick, the top layer isn't being helped through by the feed dogs and can therefore be held back in front of the foot. This will cause puckers – and the quilt to be thrown across the room! A walking foot will help to prevent this from happening because it has teeth underneath it to feed the top fabric.

Threads for Machine Quilting

There are numerous threads available for machine quilting. For the seam ditches I like to use a 50 weight matching thread, preferably cotton, but something that is not going to show. Some quilters use invisible nylon thread for ditch stitching but I'm not a fan of this. I used a 30 weight cotton thread for all the other areas. The thread in the bobbin should be the same throughout – this could be anything ranging from 30 to 50 weight, cotton or polyester, depending on the required effect. You will need to practise with the different weights and adjust the top tension accordingly.

If you choose to use a different colour thread on the back from the front, you will have to be careful that the top thread isn't showing on the back and the bobbin thread isn't showing on the front. Adjusting the top tension will overcome this. If the bobbin thread shows on the front then loosen the top tension (lower number). If the top thread is showing on the back then tighten the top tension (higher number).

You could also consider using variegated threads. They can look really effective on the front and back of the quilt and come in lots of different colourways.

Stitches for Machine Quilting

You can either use a straight stitch (lengthened to 3.0) or a decorative one, depending on where it will be sewn. I sometimes use a bridging stitch (Fig 1) for ditch quilting but have given a few other suggestions below (Fig 2). Consider what the stitch will look like if it has to cross another line of stitching or turn a corner. Practise first!

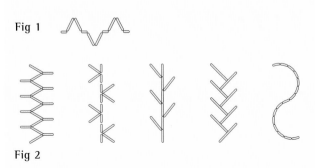

Fig 1

Fig 2

Machine Quilting Basics

- To secure the layers, place the front of the quilt right side down, the wadding (batting) on top (not for the Heirloom Quilt as this is already sewn in), and the backing, right side up on top of that. Tack (baste) the layers together, flip the quilt over so the front is on top and then safety pin the layers together.
- When layering together, don't scrub wrinkles out with your palms as this will stretch the top layer, causing the layer beneath to wrinkle. Instead, pat the layers down, beginning in the centre and working towards the edges.
- When quilting, set the machine to stop with the needle *down* in the fabric. If your machine automatically lifts the foot slightly when the needle is in the fabric, you may prefer to take this function off temporarily (in the Set or Tools menu) because the quilt is heavy and tends to move when the presser foot lifts.
- Draw up the bobbin thread to the top when you begin and either fix to secure the ends or tie them later. Bringing the threads to the top of the quilt will prevent you from machining over them and having to unravel them later. The thread tails can be knotted and then buried into the quilt using a large-eyed or easy-threading needle.
- Working with such a large, thick quilt is not easy! Always lengthen your stitch and take your time. Enjoy the process: remember, you're almost finished!
- Make sure the quilt isn't hanging and pulling over the edge of the table in front of the machine as this will prevent it from moving through and you will end up with tiny stitches. Lift the quilt up in front of the machine so it can feed through easily.
- Look at the quilt and decide on a quilting line that is near the centre and start there. Next, quilt a line that is about halfway between the centre and an edge. Do this for each side of the quilt. These lines could be going diagonally, vertically or horizontally. You need to avoid quilting heavily in one area to begin with. Look at the quilt as a whole and anchor it throughout then go back and fill in the areas with more quilting.
- When quilting in the ditch, sew on the low side (if any) as the stitches won't show as much. This is the side without the seam allowances underneath.
- Spread your hands out on top of the quilt using them like a hoop.
- Be careful if you are using a walking foot and sewing over ribbon or satin as the teeth under the foot can snag or catch. Try placing a strip of water-soluble stabilizer or tear-away stabilizer under the foot to prevent this from happening.
- You will sometimes have to sew over a large bump at the beginning of a seam (for example, the top of the Cathedral Windows). Use the Clearance Plate (it may also be called Jean-a-Ma-Jig or Hump Jumper depending on your machine) in front or behind the foot. This will prevent skipped stitches.
- Instead of quilting in the ditch, consider quilting ¼in–½in (6mm–1.3cm) away from the seam line. This is much easier and can look quite effective. Echo quilting is also very effective to fill in large areas (see opposite).

Italian Quilting

This technique is used in the Trapunto Corner block and the trapunto cushion project. Italian quilting is sometimes referred to as corded quilting and in a way is a type of trapunto because it forms raised areas in a design. The difference is that the raised areas are channels rather than shapes. See page 140 for machine trapunto. Most designs can be adapted to incorporate Italian quilting simply by drawing a second line about ¼in (6mm) away from the first design line and threading wool or cord between the two parallel lines.

1 Trace the design to be quilted on the front of the background fabric using a suitable fabric marker.

2 Pin the quilt wadding (batting) or a backing fabric (not the main backing fabric for your quilt as you will have holes in the back!) such as muslin or fine cotton underneath the background fabric.

3 Machine both layers together along the lines of the channels. If any of the lines cross, decide which channel will go underneath. Do not stitch the channel where it crosses the other one, otherwise you will not be able to thread the cord through. For a more pronounced effect, a narrow decorative cord may be couched along the lines instead of a machine straight stitch.

4 Cut a length of quilting wool the same length as the channel. For a narrow channel, slightly more than ⅛in (3mm), use one length of wool. For a wider channel, about ¼in (6mm), use a double length. Thread this through the eye of a large, blunt needle. If this is difficult, use a cradle to draw the thread through – cut a 2in (5cm) length of thread, fold this in half and push the loop through the eye of the needle. Thread the wool through the loop of thread. Pull the loop of the thread back through the needle, pulling the wool through with it.

5 Push the needle through the wadding from the back, making sure the needle does not pierce the top of the work. Begin at one end of the channel, pushing the needle through as far as you can. Leave a short tail of wool at the beginning and when you reach a corner, sharp curve or a point where the channels cross, come up for air!

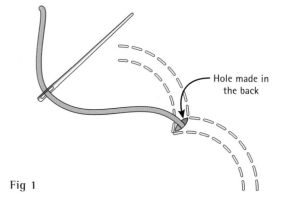

Hole made in the back

Fig 1

6 Push the needle out through the wadding on the back and pull the wool through. Leave a small loop of wool to prevent it from being pulled too tightly (Fig 2) and reinsert the needle in the same hole, gently pulling the needle and cord through. You may need to place your thumb on the wool where it is coming out of the wadding to prevent it being pulled into the next part of the channel. Continue in this way to the end of the channel. Leave a short tail at the end and cut the wool.

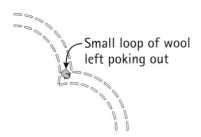

Small loop of wool left poking out

Fig 2

7 When all the channels are stuffed, clip the tails of wool at the ends of the channels. Now you can pin the backing fabric behind the wadding (batting) and background quilt as desired.

The raised effect of trapunto work and Italian corded quilting used in the Trapunto Corner block and the Trapunto Cushion are both emphasized by simple grid quilting.

Echo Quilting

Echo quilting is the term used for stitching that echoes the shape of an appliquéd or quilted design, similar to ripples on a pond. The lines are anything from ¼in–½in (6mm–1.3cm) apart and can be as many or as few as desired. The colour of the thread will usually match the colour of the fabric you are quilting. You don't always have to use a straight stitch but could experiment with a decorative, wavy, triple, or even a candlewicking or entredeux stitch. The easiest way is to simply guide the edge of the presser foot or walking foot with the edge of the shape you are echoing for the first line and then guide the edge of the presser foot against the last sewn line for the next one and so on, working outwards. However, if you want to be a little more precise, there are two methods you can use.

Method 1

At each pivot point, draw a removeable line that intersects the angle. As you sew around the shape, when you pivot on this line you will be the correct distance away from the next edge (Fig 1). This will work at whatever distance you are away from the original shape.

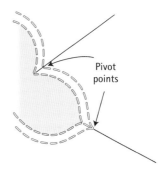

Pivot points

Fig 1

Method 2

If you want to be really fussy you can mark on your pivot points how far apart you want the lines to be. They are usually the same distance apart, but why not try gradually widening the distance between the lines the farther out you go? Marking them like this will keep everything even, which is important if you are sewing to the edge of a block and want the same number of lines all around your design.

Fig 2

Free-Motion Stippling

This is used in the borders of the Heirloom Quilt after they are attached to the quilt and before the binding is sewn. Most of the ladies who have made the quilt didn't do the stippling as they weren't too confident about the technique but they were all as happy with their quilt as the few who went the extra mile and stipple quilted. Free-motion stippling, sometimes referred to as vermicelli or meandering, takes a great deal of practise, and you'll either love it or hate it! With the feed teeth lowered on your machine, you are able to go backwards, forwards, sideways and in circles without having to turn your quilt. Some makes and models of machine have their own free-motion features – a special bobbin case, free-motion floating and a stitch regulator are just a few. In their own way these all make the process a little easier but it is still up to the user to move the fabric – which is the hard part! Think of it as drawing a design by moving the paper and keeping the pencil still.

Free-Motion Basics

- Prepare for free-motion quilting as follows.
  Lower the feed teeth on your machine.
  Attach a free-motion or darning foot.
  Adjust your machine speed to medium if possible.
  Prepare practice 'sandwiches' using a layer of calico above and below a piece of wadding.
  Thread your machine top and bobbin with any colour thread.
  Select a straight stitch with the needle in the centre. Set the stitch length to 0 to stop the teeth from turning.
  If required for your machine select the free-motion setting.
- Bring the bobbin thread to the top of the fabric before beginning to stitch. This will prevent the bobbin thread from being caught in the stitching underneath.
- Make sure you lower the presser foot. Using your practice sandwich, sew a few stitches on the spot where the threads are coming from to secure the stitching. Cut off the thread tails.
- Sew a few stitches very slowly and look at how the foot acts. When the needle goes down, the foot goes down to hold the fabric. When the needle comes up, the foot lifts up enabling you to move the fabric. Move the fabric slowly and you will find you have small stitches. Move the fabric quickly and you will create longer stitches. You will also notice that a slower speed creates longer stitches and a faster speed creates shorter stitches. Practise sewing straight lines at different speeds to see what happens.
- Look at the tension of the stitches. If the bobbin thread is showing on the top you need to loosen the upper tension by setting it to a lower number. If the top thread is showing too much on the underneath then you will need to tighten the top tension by setting it to a higher number.
- Next, experiment with how to place your hands on the fabric. There are different quilting aids that you could try, such as quilting gloves and quilting hoops and rings that are positioned on top of the quilt. I prefer to bunch the quilt up in one hand and open my thumb and index finger on the other hand to form a hoop around the stitching. With practice you will find your own preferred method.
- Before trying to stipple quilt, practise sewing up and down, sideways and in circles. Write your name and make up flower shapes and scribbles. Just get carried away, creating whatever you

want on your scrap of fabric. Don't worry about producing a perfect stitch length, or crossing over previously sewn lines. It is important to feel comfortable with the technique and enjoy the process.

- Now sew loops, or joined up 'e's, sewing them in one direction and then in the opposite direction. When comfortable with this, try to keep an even stitch length by moving the fabric and keeping the machine at a constant speed. With free-motion sewing you don't have to turn the fabric while the machine is going, just move it backwards, forwards, sideways and in circles. However, you may need to stop, adjust the fabric by turning it to a different position and start again.
- You are now ready to try stippling. Before sewing, draw stippling designs on a piece of paper – see example in Fig 1. This will give you practice in forming the design, which is difficult when the machine is going 90 miles an hour! I think it's more difficult than sewing feathers or quilting designs. You not only have to think about moving the fabric and keeping an even speed, but decide where to go and what shape to 'draw'. This is more difficult if you have to manoeuvre around small shapes and areas. Practise the shapes below, concentrating on keeping the lines curved rather than pointed. After lots of practice and when you feel ready, draw a stippling design on your fabric and free motion over the lines, to get you in the swing of the stippling pattern. When you come to the end of your drawing, continue on, making the design up as you go along – feel free and enjoy!

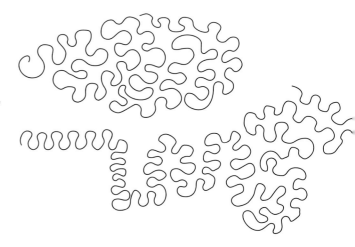

Fig 1

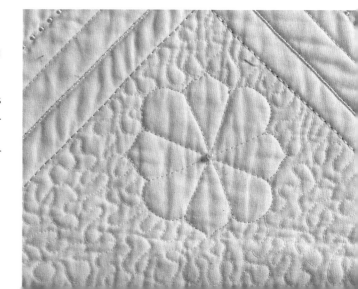

Smocking by Machine

This technique is used in the Smocking block of the Heirloom Quilt and in the Christmas stocking project. The main difference between hand and machine smocking is that a hand-smocked piece has a certain amount of stretch in it whereas a machine-smocked piece will have no give at all. One of the most authentic stitches to use for machine smocking is the triple straight stitch, programmed with different needle positions to give a wave effect. Some machines have these stitches already programmed in the machine in a variety of widths, but if not you may be able to programme these stitches yourself as explained below. Other effective stitches for smocking are the ones that work well for wing needle stitching, as these go backwards and forwards forming a heavier, denser stitch which will show up better. Dainty designs do not look as effective. Experiment with your different stitches to see which ones work the best.

For smocking it is best to use a fine, natural fabric such as cotton batiste, silk or fine satin, as it will be pleated or gathered before being stitched. A heavier fabric will be too thick. Allow approximately three times the required finished length of your piece. Most fabrics are best cut with the long edge running parallel to the straight grain (selvedge), but practise first on both grains to determine which is best.

Pleating or Gathering

For the Smocking block in the Heirloom Quilt and the Christmas stocking I used a smocking pleater. A pleater makes the neatest pleats and comes in various widths, however, they are quite expensive. Another option is to use a gathering foot for your machine, sewing the lines approximately 1in (2.5cm) apart. You may need to lengthen the stitch and tighten the tension in order for the fabric to gather well. If you hold the fabric down behind the needle, so that it bunches up, and then release it every so often, it will give a better result. When the lines have been sewn, pull the sides taut in order to straighten the gathers. Another method of gathering is to sew parallel lines of machine stitches, described below and shown in the sample below.

1 Thread your machine top and bottom with a polyester thread that matches your fabric. Polyester thread is stronger than rayon or cotton thread.

2 Draw a line on the wrong side of the strip about ½in (1.3cm) from the top of one short end. This will be the point where you begin each line of sewing and will help you keep the stitches in line so that when they are pulled up, the gathers are even. Don't worry too much if they don't line up as the decorative stitching will hide any blips! Beginning at the raw edge at one side, mark every ½in (1.3cm) along the line.

3 Select a straight stitch, length 6.0 (or the maximum length) and loosen the upper tension slightly (to a lower number). Make sure you have long thread tails before you begin. Using the regular machine sewing foot, begin at the first ½in (1.3cm) mark and sew down the strip, keeping the same distance away from the edge. Do not secure the threads at the beginning or end. Remove from the machine and cut off the thread tails leaving about 5in (13cm). Begin at the top again at the next ½in (1.3cm) mark and sew to the end. Repeat sewing lines down the strip in this way until you have filled the strip. To keep the lines parallel, either use a mark on the foot as a guide or move the needle over so that the edge of the foot is next to the previous line of stitching. Alternatively, use a seam guide (the long metal arm that came with your machine). If you still find it difficult to keep the lines straight then mark them with an air-erasable pen before sewing.

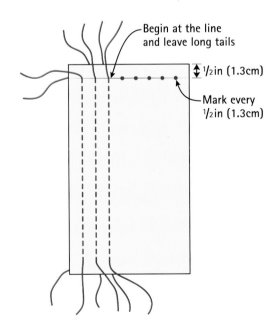

Begin at the line and leave long tails

½in (1.3cm)

Mark every ½in (1.3cm)

Fig 1

4 When all the lines have been sewn, pull up the bobbin threads so that each line of gathers measures the required length. Knot the threads with a triple knot and trim them to about 1in (2.5cm). Adjust the gathers in the strip so they are as even as possible and then pull the sides of the strip away from each other to straighten the gathers. You will have sewn the lines with the wrong side of the fabric facing up which means that the bobbin threads you pulled are on the right side of the fabric. In my opinion this gives a nicer look to the gathers. However, you decide which side you prefer when you sew your practice piece. Sew the lines with the fabric right side up if you prefer.

Preparing to Smock

The following points should help you prepare your pleated or gathered fabric for smocking.

- When you have pleated or gathered your fabric, it is important to make the lines as straight as possible. A comb or hair rake is a good tool to use and pulling the sides taut against each other will help.
- Once it is the correct size and as straight as possible, iron a piece of fusible interfacing to the back. This will keep it in place and help prevent distortion. In addition to this, use a tear-away stabilizer under your fabric.
- Lower the presser foot pressure slightly and loosen the tension a little on your machine.
- Use a 30 weight rayon embroidery thread in the top, in a colour that will show up well against your fabric, and a 50 weight thread in the bobbin.
- Attach either a transparent embroidery foot or an open-toe foot to your machine.
- Prepare two practice pieces: one flat piece of fabric and one that has been pleated or smocked the same as your main piece. You will need to decide which stitches to use on the flat piece and then practise them on the smocked or gathered piece. You will be sewing in the opposite direction to the pleats/gathers.

Machine Smocking

Begin down the centre of your panel – either mark a line using an air-erasable marker pen, crease a line, or use one of the pleating/gathering threads as a guide. Because the pleated/gathered fabric is so thick, you may need to lengthen the stitch to avoid it bunching up. Sew *slowly* down the centre of the panel and use tear-away stabilizer beneath.

Sew the next stitch either side of the centre, lining up either the edge or the inside edge of the foot against the previous row. Continue adding rows of stitches, sewing them in the same direction each time, until you have completed the required width of smocking.

Wave Stitches

A wave stitch, if not already on your machine, may be programmed in as follows – this will produce quite a wide wave (Fig 2). The following will work for any machine that has a triple stitch that can be moved left and right of the centre (by adjusting the needle position) and machines with a memory so it can be programmed. Programme as follows:

Triple straight stitch, two settings to the left of the centre
Triple straight stitch, one setting to the left of the centre
Triple straight stitch, centre position
Triple straight stitch, one setting to the right of the centre
Triple straight stitch, two settings to the right of the centre
Triple straight stitch, one setting to the right of the centre
Triple straight stitch, centre position
Triple straight stitch, one setting to the left of the centre.

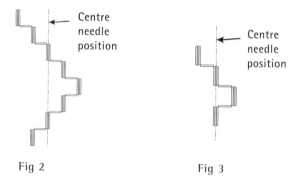

Fig 2 Fig 3

Shallower Wave

For this (see Fig 3), programme as follows:
Triple straight stitch, one setting to the left of the centre
Triple straight stitch, centre position
Triple straight stitch, one setting to the right of the centre
Triple straight stitch, centre position.

Diamond Shapes

These can be made by sewing a second line of wave stitches mirror imaged side to side. Make sure that you start at the beginning of the programme for the second row and press the 'Stop' or 'End of Pattern' button so that you can check that the stitches are lining up properly. Fig 4 shows some stitch choices but there are many more you can try.

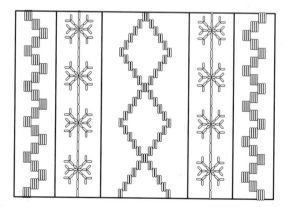

Fig 4a

Fig 4b

Fig 4c

Fig 4d

Corded Wavy Tucks

This technique is used in the Corded Wavy Tucks block and the bag project. Wavy tucks are made by 'flip flopping' sewn tucks. The edge of a tuck is sewn to the background at intervals. The edge is then folded back in the opposite direction between where it was sewn. The tucks can only be manipulated in this way if the fabric has some stretch built in to it, or is used on the bias grain.

1 You will need to sew a series of tucks along the bias grain the same distance apart. With the wrong side of the fabric up on the ironing board, use a hera marker or something similar to mark the lines, parallel to the bias (Fig 1). Fold and press a crease, wrong sides facing, along the marked lines.

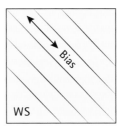

Fig 1

2 Thread the machine in the top and the bobbin with a colour matching your fabric. Keeping the wrong sides together, sew ¼in (6mm) from each folded edge. Iron the tucks flat in one direction (Fig 2).

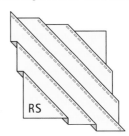

Fig 2

3 To sew the cord to the folded edges, first stretch the folded edges of the tucks using an iron. It is important *not* to sew the cord on too tightly as this will prevent the fabric from curving. Stretching the edge of the fold will enable a longer length of cord to be attached.

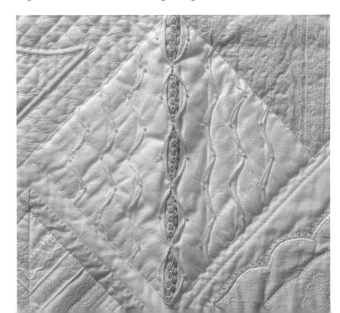

4 Select a zigzag stitch, adjusted so that it is wide enough to cover the cord, about width 2.0, length 2.0. Use a thread in the top and bobbin to match the cord. If available, use a foot that has a guide in the centre, such as an edge-joining foot or ditch-stitching foot. Alternatively, use an open-toe or narrow braiding/cording foot. Feed the folded edge of the tucked fabric on the left of the guide and the cord on the right of the guide. You may find it helps to tape a ¾in (2cm) length of a plastic coffee stirrer (or narrow straw) 1½in–2in (3.8cm–5cm) in front of the needle at about a 30° angle to the right (Fig 3).

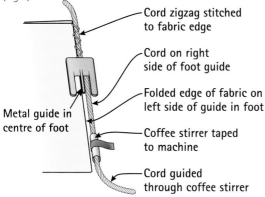

— Cord zigzag stitched to fabric edge

— Cord on right side of foot guide

— Folded edge of fabric on left side of guide in foot

Metal guide in centre of foot

— Coffee stirrer taped to machine

— Cord guided through coffee stirrer

Fig 3

5 Feed the cord through the hole in the stirrer (if using) and feed the fabric at the same angle. Begin with the needle down in the fabric before you position the cord. Without stretching or pulling the cord but keeping the fabric taut, sew the zigzag stitch so that the left swing pierces the edge of the fabric fold and the right swing goes over or into the cord. The edges should be wavy and stretched out when sewn. The width of the zigzag may have to be adjusted depending on the width of the cord and thickness of the fabric.

6 Lay the tucked shape right side up and position a ruler on top with the edge of the ruler along the diagonal that runs in the opposite direction to the tucks. Place a pin or mark on the edge of each tuck to mark the diagonal (Fig 4).

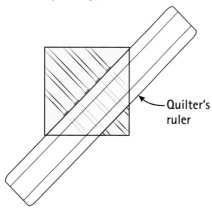

— Quilter's ruler

Fig 4

7 Move the ruler up 2in (5cm) and mark each tuck along the edge of the ruler. Continue marking the tucks in this way to the corner. Repeat for the other side of the diagonal (Fig 5).

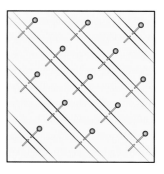

Fig 5

8 Place tear-away stabilizer underneath. Sew the edge of each tuck to the background at each pin mark with either a triple stitch or a few zigzag stitches, length 0. Secure threads at beginning and end (Fig 6). The purpose is to catch the edge of the tucks to the background.

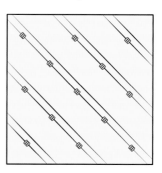

Fig 6

9 Turn back each tuck between the sewn points in the opposite direction and sew down as before (Fig 7). A bead or single decorative stitch pattern sewn at each point looks very effective.

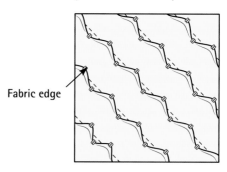

Fabric edge —

Fig 7

Cathedral Windows

This technique is used in the Corded Wavy Tucks block and the bag project. There are many different ways of sewing Cathedral Windows. The effect is made by folding back two edges that meet, revealing either a contrasting fabric, a decorative stitch, braid or lace underneath. In order to be folded back at a fold or seam, the fabric has to either have some built-in stretch or be cut on the bias.

1 Cut two squares, or required shapes, of fabric each with at least one edge parallel to the bias grain. Place right sides together and tack (baste) a 1in (2.5cm) seam along the bias edges and press the seam open (Fig 1).

Fig 1

2 Place your chosen 2in (5cm) wide strip of contrasting fabric behind the seam with the right side up. This could be embellished first with decorative stitches, braid or lace. Tack (baste) the strip in place either side of the seam.

3 Undo the basting stitches that are in the seam. On the right side, mark the folded edges that formed the seam with pins or an air-erasable marker every 2in (5cm) or your required length/distance (Fig 2).

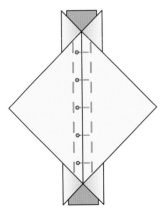

Fig 2

4 Place tear-away stabilizer underneath. Sew the seam edges together at the marked points with either a triple stitch or a few zigzag stitches, length 0 (Fig 3).

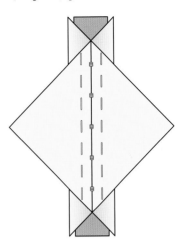

Fig 3

5 Fold back the seam edges between each sewn point away from the centre, revealing the fabric behind. Sew the edge halfway between the previous sewn points to the background as before (Fig 4). Remove the tacking (basting) stitches either side of the centre seam.

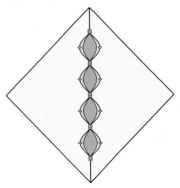

Fig 4

The cathedral windows technique can look even more eyecatching if contrasting fabric colours are used, as in the Wavy Windows Bag.

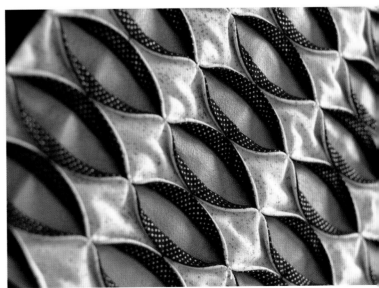

Machine Trapunto

This technique is used in the Trapunto Corner block and the trapunto cushion project. Trapunto is the name given to areas of a quilt that have additional stuffing, creating a design that stands out in high relief. Using a decorative stitch or cord couched around the edge of the design adds to the effect. There are various ways to layer and sew a trapunto design by machine. After many trials, I think the following two methods are the best.

Method 1

In this method the areas are stuffed *after* they have been sewn by making a small slit in the back and pushing the stuffing through. The slit is then sewn closed by hand to prevent the stuffing from falling out. The project must then be backed or lined. Instead of making slits in the backing fabric, a fabric such as muslin which has an open weave may be used. It is then possible to push the stuffing through the holes in the weave.

1. Mark your design on the right side with a disappearing pen or grey quilter's pencil. Place your chosen quilt wadding (batting) underneath the quilt top and either a piece of muslin or a medium weave fabric beneath that.

2. If the finished project is a cushion or one where the backing will not show, quilt any areas that are not trapunto shapes. If the finished project is a quilt or one where the backing will show, then leave this stage until after the shapes have been stuffed.

3. Sew a straight stitch, decorative stitch or couch cord around the outside of the trapunto design.

4. Using a blunt, thick needle or similar, gently push stuffing through the backing into the trapunto shape. If you are using muslin as your backing, make a hole in between the threads to push the stuffing through. If you are using a medium-woven backing fabric, you will have to make tiny slits in it, which will need to be sewn closed afterwards. You may either place the stuffing between the wadding and the top fabric or between the wadding and the backing fabric, depending on the look you want to achieve. For this method I prefer to place the stuffing between the wadding and the top layer. Be careful not to over stuff as this will distort the shape of your quilt. Once the trapunto is finished, back or line your quilt.

Method 2

For this trapunto method, the areas are stuffed first and then sewn. This may sound a little weird, but it works! As the trapunto is done before the quilting, the backing is put on afterwards and quilted in the usual way.

1. Mark your design with a disappearing marker or grey quilter's pencil. Pin either 4oz (135g) polyester or lofty wadding (batting) under the trapunto shape on the wrong side of the quilt top, making sure it covers the complete area. The thicker the wadding the more dramatic the trapunto will be, but also the more distorted the areas around it will be, so practise first to see which you prefer.

2. Using a walking foot, thread to match the quilt top and stitch length of 3.5, sew around the outside only of the trapunto shape. Use your hands on top of the fabric like a hoop, keeping the top fabric flat. When this stitching is finished, carefully cut away the excess wadding around the outside of the shape.

3. Pin the quilt wadding under the quilt top. If the finished project is a quilt or one where the backing will show, then this should also be pinned to the back of the quilt top, under the wadding. If the finished project is a cushion or one where a backing will not be attached, then iron fusible interfacing to the outside of the quilt wadding before it is pinned in place. This gives more stability and will help to prevent any distortion that may occur.

4. Sew around the outside of the design using one of the following methods:

a) Couch a decorative thread or cord using a zigzag stitch, covering the first line of stitching.

b) Sew a decorative stitch covering the first line of stitching.

c) Sew a straight stitch, unpicking the first line of stitching 1in (2.5cm) at a time, just in front of the needle.

d) Use a water-soluble machine sewing thread for step 2 above, straight stitch around the shape and then spray with water or wash to remove the soluble thread.

5. Sew any accent lines that may be on the shape and then background quilt around it. The closer the background quilting, the more effective the trapunto will be.

Making and Applying Piping

Adding piping to a project gives a very elegant and professional finish. I like to insert it between the border and the binding on a quilt but on the Heirloom Quilt I got a bit carried away and inserted piping between the edges of the quilt top and the border as well!

A contrasting fabric always looks best so that the piping will stand out. Technically, you don't need to cut the fabric that covers the cord on the bias unless you are piping a curved edge. However, when working with silk I do cut it on the bias when possible to eliminate fraying. If you need to join the strips, do so with a diagonal seam – see step 3 Double-Fold Binding with Mitred Corners opposite. The width of your fabric strips needs to be twice the width of the seam allowance plus enough to go all the way around the cord. I use 4mm wide cord and cut the strips 2in (5cm) wide. I have a wonderful gadget to trim the piping before it is inserted (called Darr Piping Magic – see Suppliers), which has grooves for seam allowances ¼in, ⅜in, ½in and ⅝in.

1 Cut the strips of fabric to cover the piping from a contrasting colour to the fabric it will be inserted between – see above. Finger press the fabric piping strip in half, wrong sides together.

2 Wrap the fabric strip around the cord so that the cord sits in the fold. Use either a piping foot or zipper foot, and move the needle over slightly to the right, away from the piping, so that the stitching line will not be right next to the piping. Doing this will prevent this line of stitching from showing when the piping has been inserted. Lengthen your stitch to 3.5 and sew to the end of the strip.

3 Trim the piped strip to ½in (1.3cm) or to your required seam allowance from the edge of the piping cord.

4 Align the raw edges of the piped strip with the raw edges of the top edge of the quilt/project. Keeping the needle in the same position and the stitch length at 3.5, sew the piping to the edge.

5 Cut the piped strip off in line with the ends of the quilt. Continue in this way, sewing the piped strip to the quilt top on all four sides.

6 Pin the binding (or fabric that will go the other side of the piping) to the edge of the quilt, right sides together. Position the needle so that you will be sewing right next to the edge of the piping cord that is sandwiched between the layers, and machine through all the layers with a 3.0 stitch length (Fig 1). The first two rows of stitching should not be showing as they will be in the seam allowance.

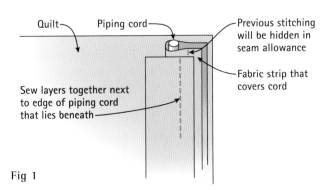

Quilt
Piping cord
Previous stitching will be hidden in seam allowance
Fabric strip that covers cord
Sew layers together next to edge of piping cord that lies beneath

Fig 1

Double-Fold Binding with Mitred Corners

A double-fold binding gives a more durable edging to a quilt than single-fold binding and will stand the test of time.

1 Before beginning the binding, tack (baste) the edges of the quilt ¼in (6mm) from the edge all round using a walking foot.

2 Cut the binding across the grain i.e., in the opposite direction to the straight grain. There is no need to cut a quilt binding on the bias unless it is to go around a curved edge. There is, however, a little 'give' in the fabric along this grain so the binding won't look too taut. Also, if using silk, it will not fray as much on this grain. The cut binding width should be six times the finished binding width plus ¼in (6mm). For ½in (1.3cm) finished binding, cut the width to 3¼in (8.2cm). The length of the binding should be the perimeter of the quilt plus about 10in (25.4cm). Join the strips with diagonal seams (see Fig 1).

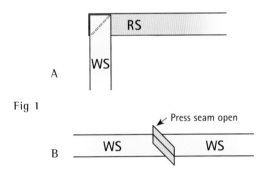

RS
WS
A
Fig 1
Press seam open
WS
WS
B

3 Fold and press the binding in half along the length, with wrong sides together. Leave about 8in (20.3cm) of binding loose at the beginning and start about 8in (20.3cm) before a corner. With right sides together, align the cut edges of the binding with the cut edges of your quilt. Using a walking foot, sew a shy ½in (1.3cm) seam allowance or a seam allowance just shy of the finished width of your binding. At the corner, stop sewing the width of the seam allowance away from the corner with the needle down in the fabric (Fig 2A). Lift the presser foot and sew off diagonally to the corner. Cut the threads and remove your work from the machine. Fold the binding diagonally up at a 45° angle and in line with the next edge of the quilt (B).

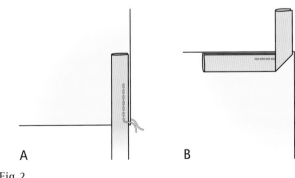

A
B
Fig 2

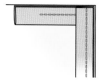

4 Fold the binding down parallel to the next side of the quilt with the raw edges matching and the fold at the top even with the first edge. Begin sewing at the folded binding at the top and continue to the next corner (Fig 3). Continue in this way, mitring all the corners until you are about 10in (25.4cm) from where you started. Remove the quilt from the machine to join the binding ends together.

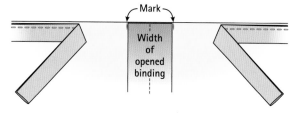

Fig 3

5 You should have an 8in (20.3cm) tail of binding where you started and another tail left at the end with a 10in (25.4cm) gap between the two ends where the binding is not sewn to the quilt. Open out the end of the binding and lay this width across the edge of the quilt in the middle of the unbound length (Fig 4). Mark the quilt with pins or chalk at the edges of the opened binding.

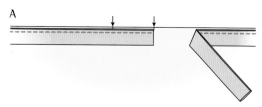

Mark
Width of opened binding

Fig 4

6 Cut the binding on the left where the right-hand mark is and the binding on the right where the left-hand mark is (Fig 5).

A

B

Fig 5

7 Place the two ends of binding right sides together and turn the binding that is on the top 90°. Join the two ends with a diagonal seam (Fig 6). Trim the seam allowance to ¼in (6mm) and press the seam open.

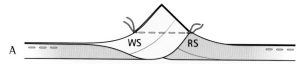

A   WS   RS

B

Fig 6

8 Put the work back on the sewing machine and finish binding your work with the joined binding.

9 Fold the binding to the back. The front should form neat mitres at the corners. On the back, tuck the fullness at the corners to the opposite side that the front fullness is on. Slipstitch the binding edge just beyond the stitching line all round.

A Final Note...

Your Heirloom Quilt is finished at last and I hope that you have not only enjoyed the process but are delighted with the results. You will find that the techniques you have learned while making this quilt will be invaluable in the future, giving you the confidence and inspiration to create many more beautiful things. One final task remains and that is to create a label for the back of your lovely quilt so all its admirers down the years will know some of the details of its creation and marvel at the skill that went into its making. Details you might include are: your name, the date the quilt was created, who it was made for or for what special occasion it was made. You could simply use a permanent marker pen to write the details on a piece of fabric and appliqué it on to the back of the quilt, or hand stitch the details in backstitch. If you own a sophisticated sewing machine you could stitch a more ornate label using machine text, perhaps adding a decorative border all round.

About the Author

Pauline Ineson has been joined at the hip to a sewing machine from a young age. She has explored all forms of machine sewing to include dressmaking, quilting, free motion, heirloom sewing and appliqué, producing many original designs and techniques. Whilst living in America for seventeen years, she ran a very successful sewing school for children. Following in her mother's footsteps, her daughter, Katie, has designed and developed her own unique children's sewing school in Worcestershire. The award-winning Heirloom Quilt is taught by Pauline at Sytchampton near Worcester where she has been teaching many other machine sewing courses for over ten years.

Acknowledgments

My thanks go to my two daughters, Laura, for pushing me to write this book in the first place and Katie, for supporting and encouraging me throughout. Also to my husband, Jim, for pretending not to notice when my fabric stash grew or a new sewing machine arrived!

Suppliers

The Cotton Reel
www.thecottonreel.co.uk
Tel: 01905 525938
For templates for cutting the Heirloom Quilt blocks to size before sewing together

Darr, Inc
www.darrsewnotions.com
Tel: 001 251 661 5191
For Darr Piping Magic gadget

Dunelm Mills
www.dunelm-mill.com
Tel: 0845 165 65 65
For roll pillow form

Oliver Twist Threads
Threads available from various outlets including
The Cotton Patch
Tel: 01904 16 6016
For stranded cord, rayon boucle and twisted rayon cord

Pauline Ineson
www.paulineineson.co.uk
Tel: 07800 822056
For most of the supplies needed for the Heirloom Quilt

Index